CULTURAL COOPERATION IN SOUTH ASIA

South Asian Regional Dialogue

CULTURAL COOPERATION IN SOUTH ASIA

The Search for Community

PAPERS AND PROCEEDINGS OF THE FIFTH SOUTH ASIAN DIALOGUE

edited by
Jamil Choudhury

MANOHAR
2000

ISBN 81 7304 346 9

First published 2000

Cover design: Ashraful Hassan Arif

This edition of the book is published in association with The University Press Limited, Dhaka, Bangladesh.

Published by
Ajay Kumar Jain
Manohar Publishers & Distributors
4753/23 Ansari Road, Daryaganj
New Delhi 110002

Fax: 326 5162
E-mail: "manohar" <manbooks@vsnl.com>

Produced by
The University Press Limited, Red Crescent Building,
114 Motijheel C/A, Dhaka, Bangladesh for Manohar Publishers & Distributors, New Delhi, India.

Contents

PART I

INTRODUCTION

PREAMBLE AND EPILOGUE TO THE FIFTH SOUTH ASIA REGIONAL DIALOGUE

Rehman Sobhan

It originated in a collective endeavour of five think-tanks in South Aisa, the *Centre for Policy Research*, India, the *South Asia Centre*, Nepal, the *Independent Planning Commission*, Pakistan, the *International Centre for Ethnic Studies*, Sri Lanka and the *Centre for Policy Dialogue*, Bangladesh to promote a greater sense of community within South Asia.

The *South Asian Regional Dialogue* has been ongoing since 1991. The first dialogue was convened by the *Centre for Policy Research* in New Delhi in December, 1991. Subsequent dialogues have been held in Kandy (November, 1992) hosted by the *International Centre for Ethnic Studies*, in Lahore (November, 1993) hosted by the *Independent Planning Commission* of Pakistan, and in Kathmandu in November, 1994, hosted by the *Nepal South Asia Centre*. The fifth and concluding *South Asia Regional Dialogue* was scheduled to be held in Dhaka in November, 1995 hosted by the *Centre for Policy Dialogue*. Regretably this dialogue had to be rescheduled on two separate occasions because of the inclement political climate in Bangladesh in 1995/96. The concluding *Dhaka dialogue* was finally hosted by the *Centre for Policy Dialogue* at the BRAC Conference Centre at Rajendrapur, near Dhaka from 25-27 February, 1997.

The four previous dialogues had addressed such defining themes as South Asian cooperation, the impact of policy reforms in South

Asia, resolution of conflicts in South Asia, the search for a South Asian identity and finally problems of governance, democracy and human rights in South Asia. Each of these dialogues organised by some of the most prestigious think tanks of the region and mobilising scholars, politicians, human rights activists, artists, policymakers and grassroots organisers encouraged free and frank discussions. The participants made a realistic effort to assess the constraints to cooperation in South Asia whilst exploring the compulsions as well as positive benefits to be derived from such interaction.

The search for community within South Asia was always seen by these dialogues as being driven by a shared inheritance from our history, geography, culture and social ethos. Recognising the enormous socio-cultural diversities of South Asia as both a strength and also a historically divisive force, the dialogues sought to explore those aspects of South Asia's cultural personality which could provide the wellsprings for sustaining a sense of community. It was recognised through these four dialogues that the compulsion to resolve disputes and cooperate within South Asia must seek its inspiration from the rediscovery of a sense of community. This ongoing search for the sources of community within South Asia finally persuaded the partners to the dialogue to focus the concluding *South Asia regional dialogue* on an exploration of notions of community inherent in the value systems shared by the people of this region. In order to understand how far our sense of community is reflected in the value systems of South Asia, the *Fifth South Asia Regional Dialogue* decided to move somewhat outside the mainstream of our previous dialogues. This dialogue attempted bringing to together some of the most creative elements in the South Asia region to explore the extent to which the world of culture within South Asia reflected the shared values of the people of this region.

In order to define the concept of values it was decided to focus the fifth dialogue on *three* enduring themes, *Social Justice and Human Rights, Women in Society and Fundamentalism and Communalism,* which are deemed to be central to the concerns of all societies within South Asia. The dialogue sought to examine how the creative imagination addresses these themes through various art forms, in our respective societies. The art forms chosen included literature, the theatre, the electronic media of cinema and television, the plastic arts of painting and sculpture and the performing arts of dance and music. The participants in the dialogue were chosen for their outstanding contribution to these respective art forms or as recognised scholars in these areas. The participants were invited to make presentations on how these three socially defining themes were perceived by the various art forms in their respective countries.

The dialogue brought together an exceptional galaxy of South Asia's most creative talents. Some of the most distinguished literateurs, playwrights, cinema and theatre performers as well as directors, painters, sculptors, dance and music artists as well as scholars of the fine arts assembled at Rajendrapur to apply their creative imagination to address the themes of the dialogue. A list of participants is presented at Annexure A. Over three days papers of considerable quality and creativity were presented and discussed with candour and passion. The papers presented at the dialogue and the essence of the deliberations on these papers captured in a paper specially prepared for this volume by the *rapporteur* of the dialogue, Prof. Ferdous Azim of the Dept. of English, Dhaka University, make up the contents of this volume reporting the *Fifth South Asian Regional Dialogue*.

The volume itself cannot hope do justice to the extraordinary fertility of the dialogue both around the seminar table as well as at the dining table, rooms and gardens of the *Rajendrapur Conference Centre*, located in the middle of the Bangladesh countryside. The cloistered calm of the locale and the relaxed environment were particularly conducive to the quality of the deliberations and the development of a sense of community amongst the participants. The discussions were punctuated by visits to Dhaka every evening. This was physically taxing to the participants but enabled them to have some exposure as to how the themes under discussion were actually addressed in the world of culture.

On the first evening of 25 February, the participants were joined by a more extended audience of distinguished Bangladeshi's to first view an exhibition of paintings of some of Bangladesh's leading artists addressing the three conference themes which was organised at the National Museum gallery in Dhaka. A selection of paintings were specially brought over from Khatmandu for the exhibition by a conference participant Ms. Ragini Upadhay, one of Nepal's leading artists whose work focused on the issue of women. Ragini made a brief presentation about her work to the participants.

The art exhibition was followed by the programme at the National Museum Auditorium, which was initiated by a poetry recitation by Shabana Azmi of poems composed by her father, the famous Urdu playwright Kaifi Azmi and also of the poems by her husband Javed Akhtar. Her recitations which carried enormous emotional power, captured the three themes of the conference. Shabana Azmi had already presented a brilliant paper at the dialogue on the theme of how the Indian Cinema looks at women which is included in this volume.

Shabana's recitations were followed by the presentation of excerpts from three plays staged by Bangladesh's three leading theatre groups, which again addressed the three themes being examined at the Rajendrapur dialogue. The theme of *human rights and social justice* was covered in a presentation of *Mukosh*, written by Bangladesh's leading playwright, Syed Shamsul Huq and staged by *Nagorik Natya Samprodaya*. The play, a Bangla adaptation of Ariel Dorfiman's play *Death and the Maiden* was set within the context of the Bangladesh Liberation War. The play performed by three of Bangladesh's leading theatre performers, Nima Rahman, Asaduzzaman Noor and Abdul Hayat was directed by Sara Zaker; Nima and Sara were participants at the dialogue.

The second play *Kokilara*, staged by *Theatre,* directed by Ramendu Mazumder, was focused on the role of *Women in Society*, represented by a solo performance by one of Bangladesh's leading theatre artistes Ferdousi Mazumdar who gave a defining performance of the status of women at three different social levels in Bangladesh. The final performance, *Pathor* staged by *Aranyak Natya Dal* written and directed by Mamunur Rashid who also stars in the play, involved the full cast of the play and explored the theme of *communalism and fundamentalism* in a performance of significant contemporary relevance; Mamunur Rashid was also an active participant at our dialogue.

On the second evening on 26 February 1997, the dialogue participants were again taken to the National Museum Auditorium where along with another distinguished gathering of Bangladeshis, the gathering was initially presented with a selection of Nepali folk songs by Kumar Basnyet who is Nepal's most distinguished folksinger who also addressed some themes from the conference in his evocative melodies. The programme of 27 February was concluded by a full staging of Tagore's immortal dance-drama *Chandalika*, staged by *Shadhana* and directed by Sharmila Banerjee. The performance by one of Bangladesh's leading dance groups was centred around two of the conference themes of communalism and the role of women.

The dialogue concluded on the evening of 27 February 1998 at the Osmany Auditorium in Dhaka. The participants and other distinguished Bangladeshi audience were captivated by an initial recitation of poems of Shamsur Rahman, one of the leading poets in the Bangla language, addressing the three themes of the conference. The audience was moved by the recitation made by Nabaneeta Deb Sen, Asaduzzaman Noor, and Aly Zaker.

The curtain on the fifth *South Asia Regional Dialogue* was brought down by a full staging of *Draupadi* written, directed and performed by Sonal Mansingh who is one of the leading exponents of Indian dance in the *Odissi* and *Bharat Natyam* style. Sonal had earlier presented a most thoughtful paper at the dialogue on how classical dance themes in India addressed the subject of women. In her solo performance of *Draupadi* Sonal gave a haunting presentation of how women, as epitomised by the timeless story of *Draupadi* in the *Mahabharata*, were treated in our society and their capacity to assert their dignity and courage in such circumstances. The presentation epitomised the spirit of the conference and presented an evocative message to the participants on how the media of dance, performed with sensitivity and passion, can project the concerns of all women in South Asia, in a form which no paper or speech could hope to achieve.

The dialogue participants were entertained to dinner each evening, first by the Foreign Minister, Mr. Abdus Samad Azad, then by Mr. Salman F. Rahman, the President of the SAARC Federation of Chambers of Commerce and Industry and finally by Mr. A.M. Anisuzzaman, Chairman, Uttara Bank, where an opportunity was provided for our visitors to meet distinguished cross-sections of Bangladesh's professional community.

On the concluding morning of the programme on 28 February, the participants were taken out on launch trip on the Buriganga where they could relax, enjoy the river and reflect on their deliberations of the last three days. The concluding message of the dialogue appeared to validate the assumption of the organisers, that the creative imagination in South Asia does indeed reflect a set of shared values as to how our various art forms view the three themes addressed in the dialogue. The various cultures and societies have their own unique forms of expression, but the underlying values, as projected by the creative imagination, remain shared.

To project this sense of cultural community it was agreed that over the next few years that a series of theatre and cinema festivals, exhibitions of painting and sculpture, dance and music concerts and readings as well as discussions of literary writings should be staged in each country. In such gatherings presentations of work from each of the South Asian countries, addressing shared theme such as women, human rights and communalism could be presented by the artistes before the various national audiences. The opportunity, for example, of five plays from different countries, each addressing the theme of women in society, being staged on successive nights before audiences, in Dhaka, New Delhi, Lahore, Khatmandu, Colombo or even before village audiences was likely to do more to project the shared concerns of the women of South Asia and to establish our shared humanity than any academic presentation on the subject. The five dialogue partners thus committed themselves to the perpetuation of the dialogue process through the collective collaboration of the cultural community of South Asia who were assigned the role of torch bearers for restoring a sense of community in South Asia.

CULTURAL COOPERATION IN SOUTH ASIA

Ferdous Azim

Culture and Ideology

Culture refers to a particular way of life, whether of a group or a people. In this sense, the cultural field covers not only the intellectual and artistic products of a group of people, but embraces all aspects of life — food habits, clothes, sports, entertainment, religious festivals and rites, notions of beauty as well as practices that determine ideas of good and bad.

The study of art and literature forms part of an analysis of cultural production, and these cultural products, both in their mode of production as well as in their dissemination, help us to define groups of people, societies or nations. The study of culture is usually coupled with the study of its ideological foundations, and brings to the fore power relations that inform and keep in place dominant societal practices and forms. The cultural arena is ideological not only in the sense that it reflects and reinforces social hierarchies, but acquires greater significance as the carrier of social values and systems. Peoples and nations use culture as a differentiating or identifying factor, as evident in the use of such phrases as 'national' costume, 'typical' cuisine or 'indigenous' music. Whole disciplines such as literature have evolved around a national or regional differentiating adjective, such as 'English', 'Bengali', or 'European' literature. The peoples of those regions are then identified through these literatures or those defining forms and thus given a 'cultural' identity.

The coupling of culture and identity has a strong ideological content, and helps to mask positions of dominance and power within the cultures that it defines. Its strong homogenising tendency, has the effect of drawing all Bengalis together, for example, under the umbrella of Bengali literature, making everyone an equal inheritor of this great literary tradition. However, what this concept fails to foreground is that participation in this great tradition and access to this literature is not the same for all, and is dependent on factors such as literacy and leisure.

Culture pervades every aspect of life. But when we define ourselves culturally, it is the products of a special or 'high' culture that are usually set aside as the differentiating or identifying factors. Take the case of a national cuisine. Eating is an everyday phenomenon, but the national cuisine never denotes the quick and meagre lunch partaken of by workers for example, but the menu of by-gone emperors and princes. Cultural identity also takes as its defining means those arenas which are set aside as somehow special, what Matthew Arnold had called 'the best that has ever been thought by mankind'.

This demarcating of culture into special areas of national or high or classical separates it from the lives of everyday people of which it is an inextricable part. Social hierarchies and power positions operate to divide culture into 'high' and 'low', 'classical' and 'popular', or 'folk' (authentic and indigenous) and 'western' (corrupt and artificial). These demarcations then divide the people according to their preferences and habits. Thus the homogenising tendencies really perform a surface function — the function of masking. In reality, culture is played out within a divided and contentious terrain, demarcating power struggles where different ideologies and concepts vie to gain dominance. That is perhaps why it is an exciting field for work and analysis, and contains the potential for effecting social change and transformation.

Feminism, along with popular culture studies, has made important contributions to this field. Feminism's study of gender relations has taught us that culture in all its forms is ideologically informed, and is the main vehicle that keeps patriarchal values and norms in place. In its first phase, feminism had concentrated on creating alternative cultural spaces, where patriarchal domination would be challenged, and a feminist ideology brought into operation. Such a space, even if it can be created, has problems. First, it has to be brought to view; it must attract and draw enough people under its aegis to be recognisable as a viable cultural space at all. Secondly, and more crucially, it presupposes that the creators of this feminist cultural space (the women and cultural activists, that is) have somehow liberated themselves from all the ideological influences of culture at large. This relationship between the special cultural space and the larger cultural arena is difficult to determine and to separate. Through its experimentations and explorations, feminist cultural studies has recognised that the cultural sphere is divided and contentious, that it does not occupy an unchanging hegemonic position, and it is within the tensions of the existing cultural scene, that challenges to patriarchy can be made and the position of women debated and restructured.

Cultural studies has been markedly influenced by the concept of postmodernism. Postmodernist cultural studies do away with the categories of high and low, and celebrate the variety and richness that cultural forms have acquired in the last years of the twentieth century. Today's cultural productions cover a large variety of forms, and take on an exploration of all the thematic and conceptual concerns of the contemporary world. A rich variety is available to the cultural consumer, as far as works of art and literature are concerned, and even in the kinds of life-styles on offer, today's citizens seem to have a wider variety of choices and trends to choose from, both in the public and private sphere. Despite this celebration, today's cultural world—postmodernist cultural production—cannot be separated from the world of commerce and finance, and the ideological dimensions that had so far formed the focus of cultural analysis, has now to take on the study of markets and commerce. Fredric Jameson has aptly called postmodernism the cultural logic of late capitalism.

Again, in this marriage between culture and capital, how is the cultural activist to work towards change? A pessimistic reading would eschew any possibility of change. But if we keep in mind the notion of the criss-crossed and contentious terrain of culture, we will be able to set ourselves the task of locating those lacunae or gaps — those points of tension — and work within them to wrench change and progress.

The Dialogue

The Fifth South Asian Dialogue on Cultural Cooperation was planned with the purpose of forging a coöperation between cultural activists in the South Asian countries. To this end, practitioners in various cultural fields — art and painting, literature, drama and cinema — were brought together in a symposium in Rajendrapur in Bangladesh from the 25th to the 27th of February, 1997. The points arising from the discussion would serve as a point of departure, and would identify the commonalities across the borders enabling cultural practitioners and workers to forge links amongst the nations. The participants represented five countries from the South Asia region — Bangladesh, India, Nepal, Pakistan, and Sri Lanka. Three themes — Social Justice and Human Rights, Women in Society, and Fundamentalism and Communalism — were identified as problematic for the region, and the papers talked of ways that cultural work could be deployed to deal with these issues.

The need for dialogue was established even prior to the meet, and it was felt that cultural unity or commonality may be a better way towards forging cooperation than political or economic considerations. The countries of South Asia are popularly believed to share a common cultural heritage. Often this statement is uttered without conviction, as an empty repetition of an established dictum. As the region is divided into different nation-states, and as much of our political history is painful and divisive, and also because of the tensions that mark the relationships between the states in the present, a cultural communication between the peoples of the various regions has become difficult and well nigh impossible. The establishment of cultural communication could perhaps help to highlight our common cultural features, creating a platform which could bring about understanding and peace in the region.

It was with a view to coming to an understanding based on common problems that the three themes were chosen. The choice seems to have been guided by a sense of opposition, giving the feeling that as the South Asian states had failed or were not actively fostering these issues, and in some cases may even be seen as the main obstacle, cultural workers would now work, sometimes with, and at others, despite the state to forge these links and to debate these issues on a regional basis. This is to be made feasible by separating culture from other aspects of the state. One of the main tasks then would be to explore how this could be possible — how the cultural sphere would make itself independent of political questions to form regional links. Secondly, the meet kept the national identity of all its participants intact — each participant representing the cultural sphere of his/her nation. It became a kind of reporting of activities, instead of a brainstorming with ideas and programmes.

The culture that was discussed and reflected in the themes attributes a humanistic tradition to South Asian culture. The difficulty of maintaining this tradition may be related to the history of humanism in this country, which can be traced back to our colonial past. How far have these values seeped into the social and political fabric of our nations? and how much do factors such as religion, region or language influence our perception of ourselves as peoples and nations? Religious differences cannot be overlooked, as they have played a crucial role in drawing the political boundaries between India, Pakistan and Bangladesh. Bangladesh marks its nationhood on a notion of linguistic difference, whereas Sri Lankan politics is riddled with ethnic conflict. People — cultural activists or not — are formed within these tensions, and when we speak of cultural cooperation, we have not only to overcome these differences, but also to take due cognisance of them. Again the kind of cultural autonomy that is envisaged is difficult to achieve and to hold on to.

The papers chosen concentrated on drawing out the themes under discussion through examining what was happening in the various fields of theatre, cinema, literature and art. As such systems of production were overlooked. For example, in the field of literary cooperation, it was absolutely essential to have discussed the publishing industry and their distribution networks. A Bangladeshi writer need not publish in Bangladesh at all; she/he may choose to publish in India. The same is true for all the other countries. There is a cultural link already in place through the publishing and recording industries. While these links may be guided by commercial and sometimes technical considerations, they can be expanded to include ideological ones. A body whose recognition grants status can be instituted, and this body can through awards and prizes, or the holding of meets and festivals, hold an influential position among the regional culture industry.

The most powerful cultural link is already in place through the satellite TV networks. This needed to be taken into consideration. Many of these networks broadcast from their headquarters in Bombay in India, and their daily fare can well be seen to form the common cultural heritage for the whole region. Given that such an influential link is already in existence, the task would now be to tap the networks for broadcasting space, where the humanistic messages of unity, justice and fair play could be relayed. Local or national TV networks have already been substantially used by 'progressive' cultural workers; now the same effort has to be made at the regional level. Moreover, the link between commerce and culture is most starkly adumbrated in this particular sphere of cultural production, and the challenge is for the 'progressive' cultural worker to place her or himself within these links.

The place and position of language needs further exploration. English was the language of the meet; but most people present did not primarily work in English. Culture and language are inextricably bound, as language determines the nature and form of the work. Again, language has been a thorny political issue within and between countries in the region, therefore a sensitive handling of linguistic unities and divisions needs to be made. Translation between the languages as well as into English was strongly recommended. The Indian Sahitya Academy already provides this service within India; it was suggested that they extend their services to other countries.

The exploration of myths, cultural or religious, was also discussed. Myths, like language, provide the staple for cultural production, and it is in the manipulation of myths that new forms of culture emerge. Though there was a general tendency to valorise the myths of classical Hinduism or Sanskrit myths as the common cultural heritage of the region, it was also interesting to see how participants talked about local variations in the mythical stories. U.R. Anantha Murthy gave the example of Pampa (a Jain poet of a thousand years ago writing in Kannada) and his use of the *Mahabharata* story to show how such variations are made. Nabaneeta Dev Sen gave examples of the manipulations of the Sita figure in Bengali *gitikas*, while Sirima Kiribamune showed how Sri Lankan art traditions had recast the figure of Hindu goddesses of ancient Indian art. These examples amply illustrated the many levels at which myths exist in society, and the many uses to which they can be put. It is against this backdrop that Sonal Man Singh's interpretation of the *Draupadi* episode from the *Mahabharata* (which was performed as part of the meet) gained significance and showed the ways that cultural myths and icons can be made to serve modern-day purposes.

However, the stress seemed to be on classical Sanskrit imagery and mythology; not enough was made of Islamic myths and stories, nor of local folk traditions. The influence of the *Heer-Ranja* stories on Pakistani film and theatre was mentioned. More on folk and fairy tales, on stories of prophets and peers, on the general cultural lore of the people would provide a richer mythological tapestry, and would point not only to the cultural commonalities, but the rich diversity that cultural workers in the region can draw from. As far as forms were concerned, papers remained very much concentrated on 'modern' forms — plays, poems (very few), stories and novels, dance, painting and cinema. Other forms, such as songs, puppet shows, pottery, *melas* — that come from the regional folk traditions can be added to this repertory. Also, the more contemporary, or postmodern art forms, such as advertisements, music videos, posters, concerts or band shows need to be examined. The culture of the South Asian region cannot be sealed off from other parts of the world either; and the dynamic aspects of contemporary cultural production is producing more areas and arenas for understanding and cooperation.

The Themes

Social Justice and Human Rights

Freedom of expression was felt to be a necessity for a dynamic cultural scene. Thus cultural production itself was seen to be dependent on the guarantee of fundamental human rights. At this point, the Bangladeshi participants expressed their curiosity about the silence of Pakistani artists and intellectuals during the 1971 War and genocide, and wondered whether it had been a result of state censorship. This brought up the question of censorship, which has been a reality for many artists in the region, who have had their works banned, censored and have even been arrested for their work. As far as state censorship is concerned, there is no doubt that the artist's duty is to protest it, and to work towards the guarantee of the freedom of speech. However, the artist's conviction is most strongly tested when it comes to protecting other's equal right to freedom of speech: of those artistic products which stand in direct opposition to the humanistic values that this dialogue sought to promote, and which continue to portray sexist, racist or communalist images. Are such images to be censored or condemned? The cultural market is awash with images, vying to gain positions of domination and influence. As cultural producers, the task is to work hard and intelligently, so that a particular brand gains currency, and drives the others out of the market. For those working to bring about change — against the grain, as it were — this is indeed a difficult task. Hence the need for cooperation, the need to know and work with others working to establish similar ideals.

State censorship is not the only curb on freedom of speech and expression. Artists and writers work within the parameters set by tradition and history, which determine both the themes and forms of expression to a great extent. Moreover, financial and economic considerations cannot be ignored. These subtler, but more pervading, limiting factors make cooperation and linkage crucial; enabling artists and writers to work together towards a common desired ideal.

Theatre seemed to be the form most concerned with the establishment of fundamental human rights in the region. Theatre workers often saw themselves as political activists, as seen in the parallel theatre movement in Pakistan and the group theatre movement in Bangladesh. In India and Nepal, street theatre also performed a similar political task. It was interesting at this point to notice the influence of Bertrolt Brecht and the use of Brechtian acting techniques in the theatrical productions of this region. The regional cultural cooperation that was being forged had already in its work borrowed from wider-flung European sources, which had mingled with local and regional political concerns to form a powerful medium of advocacy and political organisation. The desirability of cross-cultural communication can perhaps be best exemplified through this process.

Women in Society

The place of women in South Asian societies and their portrayal within cultural forms formed the main focus of the discussion. It was felt that in every country in the region women occupied a position of social subordination, and that cultural work could also be deployed to help change the situation. The participants seemed very aware of the women's movement in the region, and the work and analysis that had been done through that political process. NGO developmental activity was highlighted by the presence and oral presentation of Dr M. Yunus of Grameen Bank, who graced the occasion as a special guest. The presence of members of various women's groups in the country helped to draw out issues of women's social subordination and cultural representation.

Shabana Azmi's presentation of images of women in Indian film set the tone for the dialogue. Her video presentation concentrated on the variety of images of women in Indian cinema — from the portrayals of the pure woman or the sati-savitri figure who was contrasted with the more outgoing westernised 'vamps' in the films of the 50's and 60's, to the present-day cinema which juxtaposes many images into the figure of the female heroine. Sara Zaker added to this discussion by bringing in an analysis of the 'nayeeka', around whom the film/play revolves, and whose portrayal can be deployed towards questioning and changing society's perception of women. Both popular and classical art forms came under discussion, with Sonal Mansingh's paper concentrating on dance, and experimentations in classical dance forms (including her own) which use and reinterpret classical myths to portray a more protesting or more powerful female image. It is indeed challenging for the artist with a feminist consciousness — or the artist who wants to question/change women's cultural portrayal — to work with and around these iconographic and even fetishistic use of the female figure. How can women's sexuality be portrayed, without at the same time making her an object of the audience's gaze, or in other words, without transforming her into an object of desire. The aesthetic dimensions of artistic creativity cannot be ignored, and the aestheticisation of the female figure in art and painting, dance and sculpture, film and TV, makes it difficult to attribute agency and autonomy to the female figure. An awareness of these difficulties through a mutual cooperative process was felt to be necessary before new feminist art forms could emerge.

The position of the woman artist/cultural worker is perhaps no different from the position of women in society. Sonal Mansingh pointed out that the title of *ustad* or *pandit* is not available to women in Indian classical music or dance, and recognition for the woman artist is always more difficult and delayed. This was the experience of many women in the audience. The session included a tribute to Novera Ahmed, who emblematises the kind of neglect that women artists face, and whose aborted career can be seen as emblematic of the position of women artists in society. Taslima Nasreen was also cited as a case in point. Thus a cultural dialogue can also work towards forming bridges amongst women, enabling a discussion of the position of women in the arts and literature.

Thematic awareness of women's issues again seems to be a purview of the theatre, which has actively worked around issues of rape, dowry and other systems that keep women in positions of subordination. But what was felt to be more important than a thematic representation was the relation between cultural workers and women activists. Sara Zaker opined that women activists look on theatre and culture as an instrument, to use it to carry their messages. Artistic productions have their own laws and rules, and change according to their own demands and impulses. An imposition from the outside does not work. At the same time, as was also pointed out, artistic production which is divorced from political activism can not carry a transformative potential. It is never easily accepted, because art work by people who do not have an active role in the process of political change appears in a vacuum, and does not have the adequate links. The discussion showed that there is a need for more feminist work on culture. The gap between the women's movement and the cultural movement in the region needs to be addressed before meaningful transformative cultural work can take place.

The ideological underpinnings of culture are most strongly articulated through the deployment of women's images. Change in this sphere need not necessarily follow social change, it can equally work towards effecting and bringing about that change. But change is only possible if there is a constituency that is willing and accepting, or even actively desiring and demanding a transformation. The cultural politics that has kept women subordinated can only be challenged and changed by the wider feminist movement, which must take on consciously cultural analysis and work. Cooperation in this field involves cooperation with the feminist movement, as well as amongst cultural workers.

Communalism and Fundamentalism

This session addressed the most fraught and divisive problem in the region. Definitions of fundamentalism were established in the special oral presentation by Professor Salauddin Ahmed of the Department of History of Dhaka University, who traced the growth of religious fundamentalism to moments of political crisis. While the Islamic conquest of India had resulted in a hardening of Hindu ways and customs, the history of the subcontinent has also enough examples of harmonious intermixture between communities, and common concerns and cultural patterns across different religious communities. He identified the problem of communalism as the most persistent one in the region, and one that people were now willing to work to eradicate. The question of how this phenomenon can be expelled from our political and cultural scene gained dominance during the discussion.

On the question of definitions: Professor Anisuzamaan pointed out that the meaning of the word 'secularism' has acquired a different significance and meaning in the South Asian region. Originally meant to denote 'this-worldliness', or a separation of the church from the state, this term was used to mean religious tolerance in the South Asian region, and is applied to states which foster the religious practices and customs of all its citizens. In this slippage of meaning, the word secularism has lost much of its radical cutting edge: tolerance of all religions precludes questioning and critiquing religious systems and customs which may, and in many cases, do contradict the humanistic ideals that the meet was pushing towards, specially as regards women. However, the difficulties of being truly secular even in this limited sense of the term was pointed out in the presentation by Vijay Tendulkar, who in a very personalised paper, talked about his own upbringing and the communal prejudices that form a part of our mental make-up. The struggle to overcome these prejudices takes place both at the personal and social/political level. This paper is important because it points out how all of us are constructed within existing ideological and cultural structures, and that the desired change cannot be brought about without this intense soul-searching.

However, secular cultural and political traditions do exist in the region. Intazir Husain from Pakistan traced the tradition of Urdu poetry to show how the poet is always placed in tension and opposition to the official religion, choosing *kufr* or blasphemy as his theme over *iman* or faith. This is what makes the poet a dangerous figure: challenging, renegade, and an outsider. This radical tradition in Urdu poetry can be traced down to present-day Pakistan, with the poems of Faiz Ahmed Faiz as beacons to guide aspiring poets forward. Narrative art or fiction writing has also been concerned with the problems of communalism; and the writings of Manto stand as cornerstones in the history of partition literature. Professor Anisuzzamaan mentioned an anthology published in 1950, entitled *Dangar Panchti Galpa*, which had contained Bengali translations of 2 short stories from the original Urdu of Krishan Chunder and Khwaja Ahmad Abbas. Thus cooperative efforts in the past had been made towards establishing a society which, if it not truly secular, was definitely more tolerant of religious difference, and which would combat the strained and violent communal relations of those times. We could build on these efforts in the present to forge more such links of understanding and cooperation.

Religious sentiment and faith, however, were areas that were kept outside the purview of challenge. These areas are indeed difficult to take on board, but it is essential that we deal with them specially as far as the position of women in society is concerned. Religious persecution in the countries of the region have in the past, and continue, to centre around women and the issues of female sexuality. Hence the cases of salishi stoning and deaths in Bangladesh, or the occasional satis in India. Artists and writers have also been subjected to censorship and harassment on the basis of hurting religious sentiment, as was the case with Salman Rushdie, Taslima Nasreen or M.F. Hussein. On the other hand, many participants were of the opinion that religious sentiment could not be directly challenged, as that would merely alienate people. Examples of Gandhi and Tagore were presented as ways in which religious bigotry could be questioned, without hurting the beliefs or sentiments of the people. Again, as mentioned earlier, the relationship between what this meet was trying to achieve and the political realities of our region somehow seemed to be in conflict; and conflicting views about confronting them were presented.

As theme of cultural production, it was again drama that was discussed the most. However, videos and films dealing with the communal issue have made strong protests against the rise of religious fundamentalism as well as against communal aggression. Artists have also used their paintings for the same purpose. An example of such a painting is Rokeya Sultana's depiction of the death of Nur Jehan of Sylhet. Fundamentalist Islam ostracises art, specially the representation of the human form. When states take on aggressive Islamic identity, artists have to struggle to keep their art forms alive, as has been the experience of many Pakistani artists. On the other hand, while Hinduism encourages sculpture and painting, it does not allow playing around with established iconography, as M.F. Hussein learnt with the reaction to his paintings of the Goddess Saraswati. Religious intolerance is inimical to the production of art, and the artist has to work towards a secular society, which alone can provide a basis and support for the flowering of artistic talent and establish the artistic calling.

Recommendations and Conclusions

The meet at Rajendrapur was accompanied with nightly cultural performances in Dhaka. These performances included dance recitals, poetry recitals and painting exhibitions. Evaluating the dialogue, the participants felt that it was a good first step, but that solid measures needed to be taken to ensure the spirit of cooperation and togetherness that had been achieved. One of the first recommendations was the preparation of an anthology of South Asian writings of the last 50 years, which anthology could later be included in a course on South Asian literature and culture. Along with the recommendation of an anthology, the need for translation across the languages of the region was emphasised.

The need for cultural exchange, both at the level of performance, and in the shape of seminars and dialogues, was felt to be necessary. Video shows and painting exhibitions were also recommended. A cautionary note on expense and capability to carry on these programmes was made, pointing to the other considerations that effect and influence the course of cultural production.

The optimistic impulse behind the dialogue — that cultural unity may be forged despite political divisions — needs to be fostered and encouraged. Sustained efforts may make such cooperations viable and feasible, and we may indeed be looking forward to a period of greater understanding and harmony in the region.

THE FIFTH SOUTH ASIA DIALOGUE

Inaugural address by

Justice Muhammad Habibur Rahman

Mr. President and fellow delegates.

Our written history dates back to the second quarter of the fourth century before Christ when Alexander the Great invaded India. From the Greek chronicles we know Bangladesh was then a part of the Kingdom of *Gangaridae*. The latter appears to me to be a geographical name indicating the Gangetic alluvium. Before that our region was mentioned in Shri Lanka's *Deepabhamsa* and *Mahabhamsa*. About 544 B.C. Vijaya Singha was supposed to have sailed from Bengal shores for Sri Lanka where he founded a dynasty.

Our country became a part of many an empire, the Mauryas, the Mughals and the British. It was a part of Mughal Suba. It was a part of province of the British Indian Empire. We did never call our country a Suba or Province, both meaning a *pradesh*. We have always been calling our country a *Desha,* meaning a country, with capital 'C'.

Bangladesh emerged in 1971 as an independent country. The possibility of this country's independence was embedded and nurtured in our language. From the language movement to the liberation of the country, it is a straight road towards the fulfilment of a national destiny. There are a few countries which are known by the names of the languages spoken by the peoples. Bangladesh is lucky to have that name that evokes love, affection and admiration for the land and the people and their language.

A few days back I compared our 21st February, the Martyr's day with May day. I said that as May day was not observed for the workers of Chicago alone or for the workers of the world, but for men and women of all countries. So 21st February was not only a day for Bangla, for Bengali-speaking people or for Bangladeshi people, but it was a day of respect for mother tongues of all peoples. It was a day to be observed out of respect for human dignity.

The Fifth South Asia Dialogue is heavily programmed and it represents the irrepressible energy of Professor Rehman Sobhan.

Fellow delegates, I warn you that we Bengalees have gained a notoriety for our argumentativeness. Argumentative Bengalees are often pitied against the wise Chinese.

Our country has for centuries been a sanctuary for refugees from the West. The pre-Aryan peoples, driven by the Aryans, came and found shelter in this country. Pathan rulers, pursued by the Mughals, came to this country and settled here. During British regime the families of exiled Sultans and Nawabs and politicians lived in Calcutta. One good thing in our culture is that we have welcomed and appreciated talent with little regard to its country of origin. Neither Tagore nor Nazrul was born in this country. We have adopted one of Tagore's songs as our national anthem and made one of Nazrul's songs a marching tune.

We have not developed any political theory. A country, overrun again and again by foreign invaders had not had the poise and rest for such a reflection. But when Bangladesh emerged as an independent country in 1971 it fitted so well with our hopes and aspirations.

Fellow delegates, we have derived our value system from the proverbs and sayings of the peoples and works of writers and poets. We have learnt from Nazrul to respect the avocations of the peasants, fishermen, weavers and woodcutters. Long before the Universal Declaration of Human Rights was proclaimed in 1948 we have learned to respect human beings from Tagore, Nazrul and other writers.

Religion played, as in other country, a significant role in our country. Hinduism at one point of time covered the whole of South

Asia. Our region was rather slow to accept Aryan formalism and welcomed rather gladly Jain and Buddhist dissenters. Like Hinduism, Islam also came to this country from abroad. For various reasons the adherents of Islam consolidated themselves in the north-east and north-west of South Asia.

I have read Vijay Tendulkar's article "Muslims and I". He said that in his childhood he heard about the dichotomy between Muslims and human beings. Our situation was a little better. A question was often asked about a stranger whether he was a gentleman or a Muslim.

In 1972 we incorporated four principles in our Constitution — nationalism, democracy, socialism and secularism. Later a meaning was given to socialism and secularism was dropped. Islam was made the state religion, but it was provided that "other religions may be practiced in peace and harmony in the Republic". I just like to point it out to you that there is no constitutional requirement that the Head of the State or any other constitutional post-holder is to be a Muslim or that before taking an oath one is required to make any religious invocation.

The main provisions of the Constitution are that all citizens are equal before law and are entitled to equal protection of law, that the state shall not discriminate against any citizen on grounds only of religion, race, caste, sex or place of origin, that no person shall be deprived of life and personal liberty, and that freedom of thought and conscience is guaranteed. With these provisions, I think, we have got a substantially workable Constitution with which we can work and dream for brighter days.

Secularism, the term that we have imported from the West where it slowly emerged in a different atmosphere and only partly accepted there is often not well received in this region. Our writers have, however, rejected religious fanaticism and fighting it tooth and nail against it.

It is difficult to divine on what urge a writer writes. May be it is in সৃষ্টি সুখের উল্লাসে, in the joy of happiness of creation. Sometimes best works blossomed in difficult and oppressive situation. Blue Jazz is the soul satisfying work of the slaves.

I have said again and again against the practice of *fatwa*. God in his infinite mercy will take care of our sins and failings in the world hereafter. In this world, no one, however religious or influential he may be, has got any right to execute an extra-judicial decree like a *fatwa*. Any unauthorised execution of a *fatwa* is against the rule of law and the basic principles of our Constitution. Our writers, short film makers and cultural workers have consistently stood against any act of savagery that degrades human dignity.

We were used to be called as *bratyas*, degenerate outcastes, by the Aryans. Dissent is in our blood. I think we are more tolerant than others. We had unfortunately some incidents of religious riots in 1950 and in 1964 and in 1990, after the destruction of the Babri Mosque in Ayodhya. It is a fact that some *dangas* and *hangamas* (riots and disturbances) took place in this country and we need not pride on our tolerant attitude. But it is worth mentioning that whenever any riot breaks out in this country, the people as a whole rises to the occasion to quash it with full determination.

It is difficult for me to give any survey, even in brief, of the works done by our young authors, painters, filmmakers and sculptors. I fear I may not be able to name all the illustrious ones. I like to point out that our young men and women are having good interaction with their comrades in Delhi, Lahore, Colombo and Kathmandu. We often talk about justice for the people. I like to point out that Nepal is the only country where justice is administered in the language of the people and that is done very effectively with a finesse. One year and a few months back when I went to Nepal to attend a SAARC law conference in Kathmandu, I spoke a few words in Nepalese out of my respect for my brothers in the Nepal judiciary.

I do not think I should take any more of your valuable time. I wish the foreign delegates a pleasant stay here. I wish all the delegates a very good deliberation. I am sure we will be most benefitted from your discussions. I am grateful to the organizers of the Dialogue for inviting me to say a few words in this meeting.

Thank you all.

PART II

SOCIAL JUSTICE AND HUMAN RIGHTS

BANGLADESH THEATRE: SOME SPECIFIC PERSPECTIVES

Kabir Chowdhury

Theatre has never been a pure art form in the sense of being completely engrossed in aesthetic excellence. It has never considered itself as art for its own sake. Since the beginning of theatre it has functioned as a forum, a medium through which a society's ideas, moralities, aspirations, hopes, frustrations and conflicts were presented on the stage, commented upon, and debated. As Robert Cohen says, "Theatre has provided a stage for political revolution, for social propaganda, for civil debate, for artistic expression, for religious proselytization, for mass education, and even for its own selfcriticism". This has been more evident and true at certain times than at others, but its validity is unquestionable.

The Bengali theatre's concern with social issues was manifest from its very early days. The contemporary theatre of Bangladesh is anything but socio-politically oriented. Bangladesh emerged on the world map as an independent sovereign country only 25 years ago from today after a bloody Liberation War which caused the death of millions of men and women. The liberation war of Bangladesh showed the world and demonstrated to her own people afresh a number of things. The people of this small deltaic plain of the Ganges-Brahmaputra-Meghna river system comprising only about 1,44,000 square kilometers were heroic and noble, capable of making great sacrifice, and devoted to their language and culture. They had a strong basic commitment to the ideals of democracy, secularism and a society free from social injustice and exploitation. The ruthless and systematic exploitation of the Bengali people politically, economically and culturally by the neo-colonial Pakistani rulers, for a quarter-century, from 1947 to 1971, and the genocide unleashed on them by the Pakistani military junta in March 1971 made the Bangladesh Liberation War historically inevitable. It was a people's war in every sense of the term. The entire population of occupied Bangladesh, barring a few quislings and collaborators, rose against the occupation army. Our writers, poets, novelists, short story writers and dramatists wrote on this theme from different perspectives employing such diverse literary techniques as the realistic, the symbolic, the existentialist and the absurd. The predominant note, however, was of realism. In independent Bangladesh, of all creative activities theatre showed a particular viability and a penchant for bold experimentation. Group theatres evolved in large numbers. Playwrights and theatre-workers at various levels felt the urge to give dramatic representation not only to their experiences of the war but also to their hopes, dreams and aspirations, and later, their anger, frustration and bitterness as they saw abandoned after mid-1975 the basic values associated with the freedom movement and the liberation war leaving the vast majority of the citizens in the same doldrums as before. The lot of poor people showed little improvement. The social and economic disparity between the rich and the poor grew instead of diminishing. Instead of democratic values, authoritarianism and bureaucratic overlordship became the order of the day resulting in the denial of social justice and violation of human rights as far as the common ordinary people were concerned. Secular values were deliberately throttled by fanatical mullahs and militant fundamentalists, aided by unethical power-hungry political groups and ruling cliques. Corruption became pervasive. Violence dominated the educational campuses. In the rural areas women became special targets of repression. These and some other evils that plagued Bangladesh provided its theatre activists ready material for fashioning them into plays which through meaningful innovative productions aimed at both entertaining and enlightening the audience. In the contemporary plays of Bangladesh, in fact in most of the plays staged in Bangladesh from the early 70s to date, one clearly sees the serious and prompt reaction of its playwrights to social realities, be it the position of women, the rise of fundamentalism and communal feelings, absence of social justice or violation of human rights.

I referred earlier to the vitality of our theatre. One sees it in the diverse issues it addresses thematically and in the stylistic paths it pursues. This is evident in the original plays written by its dramatists as well as in its adapted and translated ones from the rich storehouse of the world theatre. Let me now speak of some specific plays of Bangladesh to give you an idea of how our playwrights have addressed the specific issues with which our conference is concerned. But before doing it let me draw the attention of the participants to the close interrelationship of the three themes of our conference. In our society today the denial of social justice and violation of human rights often result from the activities of communalists and fundamentalists and often the most cruel victims of the above are our women. Of course there are other evil factors besides those of communalism and fundamentalism that contribute to social injustice and violate human rights in Bangladesh, such as the ruthless exploitation carried out by the rich and the powerful who include corrupt politicians, arrogant bureaucrats, greedy businessmen, rural landlords and village headman with feudal propensities. Their victims also embrace other underprivileged persons of our country besides women, among whom are landless peasants, overworked and underpaid urban workers, slum-dwellers and children. But for the purpose of the present seminar we shall concentrate on the specific issues referred to earlier.

During the last twenty-five years or so our theatre has been enriched by the works of several talented playwrights among whom are Abdullah Al Mamun, Mamunur Rashid, Syed Shamsul Huq, and Selim Al Deen. In their plays they have all thrown light on the condition of women in our society, the role and deeds of fundamentalists and communalists, and the continuing denial of social justice and violation of human rights that effect the lives of the majority of our people, producing not only much individual misery but also great social tension. Our playwrights treat of the above themes sometimes explicitly where their messages come out loud and clear, sometimes in a veiled manner and with a muted voice. But their concern with these issues is unmistakable.

Let me start with the issue of fundamentalism and communalism. Historically Bangladesh has been a secular land with a long and rich tradition of humanism and communal amity. Various religions co-existed here for hundreds of years in an atmosphere of harmony and mutual tolerance. But during the last part of the 19th century and the first half of the 20th this atmosphere was vitiated. The British with their colonial-imperialistic policy of divide and rule, a class of Hindu landlords with their exploitative machinations against the poor, hapless Muslim peasants, and a special brand of revivalist Muslim politicians with their absurd two-nation theory weakened the prevailing spirit of liberal humanism and brought about a marked decline in the atmosphere of religious tolerance and communal harmony. It was in this background that the new state of Pakistan was born, comprising two far-flung wings separated by a thousand miles of foreign territory.

From the very start religion was turned into a handmaiden of politics in Pakistan which provided the objective conditions conducive to the growth of fundamentalism and communalism. But not all over Pakistan. The eastern wing of the country which later emerged as the independent Peoples Republic of Bangladesh in December 1971 refused to abandon its humanistic secular traditions. A significant section of her people resisted the inroad of fundamentalism. The resistance took many forms: literary, cultural, social and political.

However, narrow sectarian politics and motivated use of religion among the poor and illiterate people of this region kept alive the virus of fundamentalism and communalism among a small but well-organized group of fanatics. When the people of this region started their freedom struggle imbued with the spirit of Bengali nationalism forgetting their separate identities as Muslims, Hindus, Buddhists or Christians, the Islamic fundamentalists and the diehard communalism ranged themselves against the freedom struggle of the people. They aligned themselves with the genocidal Pakistani occupation army, described the freedom movement of Bengalees of this region as a plot of India and the Hindus to destroy the Islamic state of Pakistan, and called all Bangalees who supported the liberation war Kafirs.

The Jamaat-i-Islami Party headed by the infamous Gholam Azam actively collaborated with the occupation army of Pakistan and was responsible for the killing of innumerable innocent Christian men, women and children and for the raping of thousands of helpless women, Muslims and Hindus, young and old, although the fury of the bloodthirsty beasts was specially directed towards the Hindus. The activities of fundamentalists strengthened the faith of the Bangalees in secularism. They clearly saw the extent of the havoc religion caused when it was made a tool of politics and state power. They were convinced that religion should be kept apart from the state and the government and made a matter of the individual and his personal conscience. As a natural follow-up of this thinking the first Constitution of sovereign Bangladesh framed in 1972 declared secularism as one of the four fundamental principles on which the country would be run. If we could uphold it fundamentalism in Bangladesh would have received its deathblow. But we could not. The counter-revolutionaries refused to accept the idea of a secular and people-oriented democratic Bangladesh. Aided by conspirators at home and abroad they went on plotting and in mid-1975 managed to kill Bangabandhu Sheikh Mujibur Rahman, the Father of the nation, paving the way for the resurgence of fundamentalism here.

All the governments that came into power after mid-1975 assisted the communalists and the fundamentalists not only in being rehabilitated but also in getting into positions of power and authority. However, the fight against the fundamentalists also went on in various ways. Writers, cultural activists and well-known intellectuals devoted themselves to exposing the machinations of these evil forces and urged the people to resist them effectively. This was urgently called for, as the fundamentalists had stepped up their repressive measures, specially against helpless women in the rural areas.

Let me cite some examples. In April 1992 a village *salish*, adjudication council of village elders and mullahs without any legal backing, sentenced a 14 year old girl to 100 lashes accusing her of adulterous conduct. As a matter of fact she was raped by a village elder and had become pregnant. The mullahs decided that since there were no witnesses to the alleged rape, the accused village elder could not be held responsible. They argued that under Muslim law four adult male Muslim witnesses were required, who had seen the illicit performance and would confirm the act of rape. Since no witnesses were found the girl was sentenced to 100 lashes.

In January 1993 a young woman in Chhatakchhari, Sylhet was buried in a pit upto her waist and stoned 101 times. She was about 20 years old, and had taken a second husband after getting a divorce from the first. But a local salish, led by a village mullah who allegedly had wanted to marry the girl himself, found the second marriage of the girl illegal under Muslim law and passed the cruel inhuman judgment of stoning her publicly. The girl, Noorjehan by name, survived the ordeal only to commit suicide later out of shame and humiliation.

In May 1993 another young woman of a village in Faridpur was sentenced to death by a village salish on charges of adultery. She was tied to a stake, doused with kerosene and burnt to death.

In September 1993 a salish in Satkhira, dominated by fundamentalists, found a 16 year old Muslim girl guilty of promiscuous relationship with a Hindu boy. She was sentenced to public flogging of 101 lashes and later committed suicide unable to bear the humiliation.

Besides these inhuman acts the fundamentalists declared a number of progressive intellectuals who championed the cause of secularism, freedom of thought and women's liberation. as *murtads,* i.e., apostates, killing whom constituted an act of piety. The fundamentalists got the support of greedy businessmen, profiteers, blackmarketeers and power hungry corrupt politicians. Scores of plays were written where the above realities were portrayed most vividly. In many cases one could identify the villains in real life busy planning and implementing their nefarious programmes. The Noorjehan tragedy of Sylhet inspired more than one play.

It would be relevant at this stage to refer specifically to one of our recent plays that deals with the issue of fundamentalism. Abdullah Al-Mamun's *Meraj Fakirer Ma* (The mother of Meraj Fakir) has an interesting plot. It raises some basic issues, too. The setting is a conventional rural area of Bangladesh with its normal share of poor and illiterate villagers, selfish touts and religious leaders. The mother is the central character of the play. She is sweet-natured, tolerant, loving and very fond of all her children, particularly the sons, who are different in their temperaments, attitudes and beliefs. Meraj, her eldest, is an orthodox Muslim who insists on the strict observance of the rituals of religion and patterns of conduct prescribed by Islam, such as the wearing of veil by all the female members of his family, especially by his own wife. He is a professional 'fakir', a religious teacher and has quite a few disciples, but he has a rival and competitor in the village. Among other things, this rivalry contributes to the development of the story. In spite of being fanatically disposed Meraj is not really a bad person at heart, a fact that comes out convincingly at the close of the play. Meraj has a younger brother with modern education and enlightened views. He has married a city-bred girl and they do not live in the village. However, they come to their village home from time to time when the mother has to exert all her ingenuity in maintaining peace and harmony at home, particularly in the relationship of Meraj with his emancipated sister-in-law. The father, an easy going man, is totally dependent on his wife whom he obviously adores. In spite of Meraj's indiosyncracies and conservatism it is not an unhappy home. But a strange fact of many years ago suddenly comes to light upsetting everything. Meraj's mother was a Hindu girl, daughter of the owner-manager of an opera party, where a talented Muslim youth worked as a member of the troupe. The youth fell in love with the manager's daughter. They got married and moved to a different place. Alorani became Alo-Bibi. Husband and wife lived happily and in deep contentment and raised a family. Everything went on smoothly and the family faced no serious problems. Till the above revelation. To make matters particularly disturbing it was alleged that Meraj's mother was never converted in accordance with the prescribed Islamic rules and so she was still a Hindu. That she had been living her life as a loving decent human being all these years was considered of no consequence. It was a golden opportunity for the rival fakir to push Meraj out once for all. He roused the villagers against Meraj and his mother, accusing the latter of living adulterously with Meraj's father since their marriage was not valid according to Islamic laws. A *fatwa* was given to that effect and Meraj's mother was sentenced to be stoned. Through all these events the mother retained an astounding calm and detachment, although Meraj was terribly upset. It seemed to him that all those years he was living in a home of cards that had suddenly collapsed. A terrible fury gripped his heart and he rushed home brandishing an unsheathed sword, determined to kill his mother and perhaps, himself later, and rid himself of his sinful existence. Oh, how he loved his mother and this was what she had done to him. In the climatic moment, however, his love for the mother who had borne him, given birth to him, nourished and raised him won. All the rituals and conventions of religion dwindled into insignificance. A veil seemed to be ripped off Meraj's perceptions. Humanism triumphed. Meraj threw away his sword and embraced his mother with tears in his eyes. We see in the final scene of the play Meraj gathering together the enlightened section of the villagers and leading them to the spot where his mother is buried to the waist and is about to be stoned by some villagers driven to frenzy by the fundamentalist exhortations of the rival fakir. Seeing the militant attitude of Meraj and his companions the latter bow down their heads in defeat and the play ends happily emphasizing the superiority of love and human relationships over the dry formal doctrines of religion and impersonal rituals. Meraj asks his mother's forgiveness and says that he has committed many ungodly acts in the name of religion. From now on he will cleanse himself, give up his doctrinaire preaching, and refrain from interpreting religion wrongly. The concluding words of the play come from the mother. "Remember, you have given me your word. Never indulge in any ungodly act. Serve mankind, that is the true religion. The religion of Allah".

Communalism, its exploitation by pseudo-religious village leaders for serving their own selfish interests, the evils caused by superstition, the plight of the minority community members etc. are recurrent themes in our theatre. In Mamunur Rashid's *Pathar* the issue of fundamentalism is quite explicit. Among other things the play projects the unhappy situation of the Hindus, the victims of communal strife, in a Bangladeshi village where a 'Peer' attains power through chicanery and fraud. A piece of stone near a Hindu temple is found by a villager. It is said to be a sacred relic. The idea is to grab the land attached to the temple. The situation gets tense, communal riots break out, killings take place and the leader of progressive forces in the village, a Muslim, who was in jail so long is released. He tries to restore peace and communal harmony. He addresses a meeting of the villagers and says with deep emotion "Dear villagers, for hundreds of years we the people of this Bengal have been living together along the banks of the Padma, Meghna and Jamuna. We enjoy our festivities, our Eid and Puja, together and in harmony. When we are besieged by floods and famines then, too, we stand by each other as brothers". At this point suddenly a shot is fired by some assassins and the speaker falls down dead. Utter confusion prevails and through all this the villain again comes out on top. The chairman of the village is arrested and an innocent nightguard is victimised. An uneasy calm is established. The temple survives but the Peer's influence is on the ascent. Will the Hindus be able to continue to live here after all that happened?

The play clearly evokes memories of the Babri mosque incidents of India. The situation here is reversed and presented in a deliberately low key, but the secular, anti-communal and antifundamentalist note is unmistakable.

There are a number of other plays where this theme is treated of, but not as the central concern of the playwright. Syed Shamsul Haq's *Payer Awaz Pawa Jai* and Selim Al Deen's *Keramat Mongal* clearly come to my mind. Before I move away from this topic let me just state that the issue of fundamentalism and communalism has been dealt with in our theatre time and again, sometimes directly and explicitly, sometimes tangentially, metaphorically and through innuendoes.

Now let us turn to the treatment of the issue of women in our society in our theatre. There again we have several plays where this issue is dealt with directly and several other plays where it is dealt with indirectly, but we always find that they vividly portray the true state of women in our society. We find that they are dominated, repressed, discriminated against, looked down upon and denied their due rights — human, social and economic. This is true irrespective of their class situation, although the poor illiterate rural women are the worst sufferers. We see women's freedom curbed in the name of religion. We see them as cruel victims of fundamentalists and dowry-hunting brutal husbands. We see that there is always a double standard, one for men and another for women. This embraces all areas of life — pay for work performed, punishment for moral lapses, liberty for social mixing etc.

Let us look at the play called *Kokilara* (The Kokilas) by Abdullah Al Mamun which shows us three women in three different situations. They all bear the same name, Kokila, and each is oppressed, duped, denigrated and exploited by individual males and by the male dominated society as a repressive power. Irrespective of the different social positions of the three Kokilas each is a victim of male injustice, insensitivity and oppression. The first is an innocent unsophisticated unlettered village girl who comes to the metropolis to work as domestic help in the house of a middle-aged couple belonging economically to the middle-class. This simple first Kokila succumbs to the love talks of the young nephew of the master, a university student, who promises to marry her. She gives in to the youngman's insistent demands and finds out in due time that she is pregnant, only to be abandoned by the youngman who simply vanishes. A common enough story. When Kokila's pregnancy is discovered she is charged by the mistress of the house as a whore who entrapped an innocent youngman, the son of a gentleman, by her seductive wiles. She is a shameless hussy, a whore. "What would happen to the good name of the family now? People might even suspect the master ...". The poor simple girl learns almost overnight the rules by which this so-called civilized educated society is governed. She is unbearably hurt. Out of sheer anger and vengefulness she plants the seed of suspicion about her husband's sexual infidelity in the mistress's heart. Kokila threatens the master that unless he brings back the real culprit, his nephew, and makes him marry her she will tell the mistress that he is the father of the child she is carrying. But she is no match for her sophisticated enemy. The master lays a trap, accuses Kokila falsely of theft, gets her arrested and thrown into prison. Broken-hearted, totally frustrated and disillusioned, losing all hope and faith in man or God she finally commits suicide.

The second Kokila belongs to a higher class of society that the first. She is a housewife, simple and trusting. She is not unlettered like the first, and she is full of piety, and is devoted to her rich businessman husband. With her two grown-up daughters, her education, her social status and her tireless performance as a wife and mother she is just one of the thousands of such women in our society who are hardly aware of the meaninglessness and indignity of the lives they lead. The husband of the second Kokila is a typical male of our society who takes his wife for granted and is totally unaware of her emotional needs. First he begins to ignore her and at one stage he divorces her to marry his young and attractive secretary. Kokila, instead of rising up in rebellion, remains slavishly submissive to her husband to the last, pleads with him, even begs him to let her live with him as his wife with an inferior status. With her humiliating importunings she brings about a situation where the husband can brutally say that he is a cheat, a swindler, a scoundrel, that he is tired of her, of seeing her face in the same room day after day, that he is eager to bring variety into his life, and he will do it, for he has the power to make it happen.

The third Kokila belongs to a different category. She is a lawyer, a career woman, who demands justice for the two other Kokilas. She asks for punishment for the men who wronged her clients and ruined their lives, the first Kokila's and second Kokila's. She pleads eloquently but does not succeed in obtaining justice because the dispensers of justice are men and also because she herself is a woman. The court announces that the charges brought against the accused have not been proved and so it acquits the alleged offenders honorably.

The criticism of the hypocrisy and false values of the society is obvious. There is also perhaps an implied satire on the legal system itself.

Abdullah Al Mamun's *Subochon Nirbashane* (Good maxims in exile), Syed Shamsul Haq's *Khatta Tamasha* (Sour Fun), Selim Al Deen's *Joibati Kanyar Mon* (The Young Maiden's Heart) and many other plays show the particular predicament and vulnerability of women in our society. In Syed Haq's play, *Payer Awaj Pawa Jai*, set in the background of the Liberation War of Bangladesh, we find the daughter of the village headman being made over to the military captain for ensuring the safety of his own life and property. Towards the end of the play the poor violated girl in a frenzied mood, brought on by her shame, anger and realization of the uselessness of her life, comes out of her home and bitterly castigates her father's hypocrisy and concern for his own self without thinking of his own dear daughter. She is no longer a shy and obedient village belle, but a new character who does not hesitate to speak about her own violation. She makes it clear that she has been exploited both by religion and the norms of society established by man, to be more specific the male. But she finally established her identity as an individual even at the cost of her life by committing suicide. In Mamun's *Subochon Nirbashane* we find a young woman accusing her father for the false useless maxims fed to her since her childhood, such as, peace, happiness and harmony of a home solely depend on the woman, that she has always to be patient, submissive and forgiving. But in the end her life is in shambles and she realizes that she has been a victim of age-old man-made dictums, and is now a mental cripple, incapable of fighting against all the various forms of domestic and social exploitation.

The issues of social justice and human rights feature prominently in practically all our contemporary plays. Sometimes satiric portrayal of profiteers, bureaucrats, mullahs and politicians who are responsible for social injustice and violation of human rights predominates. Sometimes the setting is rural. Sometimes both the portrayal of the villains and the setting are different. In Abdullah Al Mamun's *Akhono Kritadash* (A slave still) we see slumdwellers, rickshaw-pullers, women in various conditions of suffering and hardship, pimps, touts, a licentious religious hypocrite, hired goons, in fact, a wide panorama of events and characters that demonstrate our theatre's concern in and treatment of the theme under consideration.

Mamunur Rashid's plays like *Iblis* (The Devil), *Ekhane Nongor* (Here we anchor), *Ora Kadam Ali* (They are the Kadam Alis) also deal with the issues of social justice and human rights. The theme of class struggle is central to Mamunur Rashid's works. The playwright in his introduction to the printed version of *Ora Kadam Ali* says that he has tried to present there an ordinary picture of our class-ridden society. The characters live in this society in a dialectical relationship and the picture of the society he presents is a war-devastated one and the war is continuously spreading. The play ends on an optimistic note, as we see the exploited underdogs, the victims of social injustice, banding together and putting up a united front against the exploiters.

Abdullah Al Mamun's *Akhan Duhsomoy* (Bad Times Now) and *Senapati* (The General), Syed Huq's *Ekhane Akhon* (Life here at present), Selim Al Deen's *Sangbad Cartoon* (News Cartoon) and many other plays of Bangladesh show our theatre's concern with the issue of social justice. Many plays portray the sufferings of the poor and the underprivileged in our society which result from the machinations of several kinds of ruthless exploiters. The latter care little for social justice and human rights. Our theatre is, perhaps, too much concerned with these thematic issues and not enough with the need for attaining artistic excellence in the matter of form and technique. This is not to say that we do not have some excellent plays where content and form coalesce to create a satisfactory product but, frankly, we often find the social, economic and political views voiced there take on a strident note and an overtly propagandist character. Our theatre workers are aware of this and we are hopeful that in the coming years we shall have a fairly large body of plays where the issues of fundamentalism and communalism, women in society, and social justice and human rights will be dealt with both as weapons for social change and appreciable aesthetic creations. It seems to me that the above issues are going to demand our determined and committed attention for a long time to come at the level of our daily lives. Our theatre, too, will continue to address these issues from new angles and perspectives, employing innovative methods and techniques. I am sure awareness of and interaction with what is being done in the field in other countries of South Asia, where these issues are no less alive and vital, will be of great interest and benefit to us.

And on this note let me conclude my paper and thank you for your patient hearing.

Social Justice and Human Rights: Reflections in Bangladesh Literature

Anisuzzaman

It is difficult to conceive of a period in Bengali literature when the themes of social justice and human rights were not reflected in one way or the other. These concepts have undergone a lot of changes with time and so have their reflection in our literature. Some of our earlier poets, living probably around the tenth century, regretfully pronounced that 'the thief and its captor are the same person' or 'the jackal constantly fights the lion'. The novelist Bankimchandra Chatterjee (1838-94) had, under the influence of Auguste Comte and John Stuart Mill, published a pamphlet on equality in 1873 where he talked of inequality and injustice in the relationship between the rich and poor, the landholder and peasant, the man and woman. Although he later retracted the work, he did not withdraw such other pieces of his writings where he argued that since the right of conquest had been conceded by all, the right of theft should similarly be acknowledged. Rabindranath Tagore (1861-1941) had a great deal to say, among others, about imperialism, aggressive nationalism, autonomy and self-rule, and the position of women in society. In one of his most well known poems, he asks God:

> Have I not seen secret malignance strike down the helpless under the cover of hypocritical night?
>
> Have I not heard the silenced voice of Justice weeping in solitude at might's defiant outrages? ...

Choked is my voice, mute are my songs to-day, and darkly my world lies imprisoned in a dismal dream .and I ask Thee, O Lord, in tears: 'Hast Thou Thyself forgiven, hast even Thou loved those who are poisoning Thy air, and blotting out Thy light?'

Kazi Nazrul Islam (1899-1976) had produced a whole bunch of poems under the title of *Samyabadi* (The egalitarianist) where he scrutinised the discriminations all around. The writers of 1930s and 1940s had carried the themes further.

One notices that the question of social justice has evolved around certain issues some of which will be later discussed here more fully, like those of gender and communal conflict. The discrimination between the rich and the poor, the urban and rural people, between the high and mighty and the downtrodden and helpless has been a recurring theme in our literature. Sufia Kamal (b. 1911), the senior-most of our literary figures, nearly follows Tagore in her prayer:

Listen, O God
Listen to my entreaty for once.
Can you tell me
Why in this beautiful world of yours
There is so much misery,
Why the piteous groans of tortured humanity
Fill the sky and the forests and the hills?

The pain and the sufferings
Make the world quake,
And salty tears surge in her two eyes.
But you are calm, quiet, silent and undisturbed ...

How man showers cruelties upon man
And indulges in tortures and injustices galore!
How passionately he tries to imprison truth
In the meshes of vicious falsehood.
Sordid ugliness and horror
Bore their teeth in a horrible grin,
While your beautiful mother-earth shrieks in fear,
And a dull pallor creeps all over her adorable body.

(Translated by Kabir Chowdhury)

Abul Hossain (b. 1922) compiles a list of misfortunes that befall his hero:

The storm destroys my crops now and again,
The rudder breaks, and the sail is torn at the Meghna,

Hut after hut is submerged in flood-water.
And in cities the leaders clash,
The paddy is washed away by the river,
The pulse disappears, cloth is not available,
The winter comes with the bite of a tiger,
And the bitch of a wife gives me a child every year.

Life nevertheless goes on. I baffle my enemies
And go on increasing the tribe.
Whether I will be mentioned in your poem
Or not is beside the point. Let me enter the harvest-field
And appropriate whatever is within my grasp.

(Translated by Abu Rushd)

The desire to appropriate what he thinks his share denied cannot, however, be fulfilled due to the interplay of social forces. This gives rise to social tensions and rebellions, as Hasan Hafizur Rahman (1932-83) notices:

A procession there was,
Of gory resistance throughout. ...

I see today just one face
In the procession, as if
All faces of martyrs have
Transformed into the quintessential form in this one face.
Just one face is conspicuous,
With courage and sacrifice written large on it
This face in the procession
Is like a flag fluttering in the air
Holding up rights sovereign,
Sovereign like the sun.

(Translated by Mohammed Ali)

We shall return to the question of rights later. What is of importance at the moment is to notice that the face appears to represent courage, but not achievement, sacrifice and martyrdom rather than victory and fulfillment. That is why Hasan, in another poem complains of his country:

What you relish is death
Nothing else flatters your palate.

In your careful chronicles
There is room

Not for men of courage,
But for martyrs alone.

(Translated by Mohammad Ali)

I do not think that the poet is being pessimistic here. His wide experience has taught him to be apprehensive, his perception has led him to look beneath the surface, perhaps, deeper into the locus of power.

This, of course, is more elaborately treated in fiction. One of the best expositions of the matter is found in Syed Waliullah's (1922-71) *Lal Salu* (1949). Like most of our early novels it has the countryside as its background. The central character, Majid, wanders into a village where there are more caps than crops. He transforms a crumbling grave into a shrine, draped with red fabric, a sign of its holiness. He fully exploits the religious sentiment of the people to his own benefit and cleverly destroys all attempts to challenge his authority. Khaleq, the landed farmer and virtual head of village, whose influence is affected by Majid's entry into the scene, finds it convenient to work hand in hand with Majid, even when the latter forces Khaleq to divorce his wife. Together they concentrate all powers in their hands and are able to play with the lives of the others. Only Jamila, Majid's young second wife, refuses to be humbled by her husband who chastises her nonetheless. In his second novel, *Chander Amabasya* (1964), Waliullah portrays Quader, son of a well-to-do family, who has become a dervish. Arif, a tutor in their home, follows him on a moonlit night, lost his track, and after a while, discovers the murdered body of a young woman. Later, Quader makes Arif help him dispose of the body. The knowledge of the crime weighs heavily on Arif's mind and his attempts to tell the truth, after being arrested for the crime he did not commit, do not help him. Quader had asked him once what would he gain if he (Quder) is hanged. The police now warn him not to try to harm Quader. And a bewildered Arif keeps on asking himself: what difference does it make to the murdered woman as to who gets punished?

Undoubtedly, Waliullah does not limit himself to the social issues in this novel. He focuses, in his typical fashion, on the individual and here the introspection of individual takes him far away from gruesome reality. Some other novelists tend to emphasize the social background in which the individuals play their role. Abu Ishaq's (b. 1926) *Suryadighal Bari* (1955), Showkat Osman's (b. 1917) *Janani* (1958) and Shahidullah Kaiser's (1926-71) *Sareng Bau* (1962) portray the struggle of the downtrodden for existence. The protagonists in all the three novels are women — widowed, divorced, or deserted, even if temporarily, and are thus doubly disadvantaged in a male-dominated world. Dariya Bibi in the first mentioned novel becomes a victim of lust of the newly rich Yaqub and ultimately is driven to commit suicide. Jaigun, in the second one, is prevented from earning, even by selling eggs, because it contravenes the law of purdah, and finally forced to leave the village for an unknown destination. Only Nabitun in *Sareng Bau,* succeeds in driving away the unwanted suitor and in increasing her charm though she is undernourished.

Many of the characters in our novels consider education as a means of improving one's lot. There is, however, a great deal of debate over the merits and demerits of madrasa education and general education, on the one hand, and that of female education, on the other. In *Lal Salu*, Majid prevents Akkas from founding a school and makes others contribute to establish a mosque instead. It is clearly perceived that education cannot be easily and equally available to all in view of the discrimination between the urban and rural areas, between men and women and between people with means and those without. A combination of factors, of which education is one, makes people leave their village for the city with (to borrow a phrase from Hasan Azizul Huq (b. 1939), one of our foremost writers of fiction), tears in one eye and avidity in the other. Thus the countryside is gradually replaced in our later novels by the city which shapes out as the real centre of power. Several novels of Syed Shamsul Huq (b. 1935) deal with this change and, more particularly, with the life in city which liberates people in many ways, bounds in many other ways, but which continues to be unequal. The liberation of Bangladesh makes the city even more powerful and different.

Yet Bangladesh is predominantly a rural land. Hasnat Abdul Hye (b. 1939) notes in his novels, *Timi* (1981) and *Mahapurus* (1982), that power-structure in the countryside has not undergone any significant change, despite the country's liberation. Landholders secure elective offices — the chairmanship of Union Council, for instance, — and also the blessings of government officials. Shahed, a teacher in a rural college, who is the central character in *Timi*, realises that the villages are not as idyllic as they are portrayed in literature, and life becomes quite difficult with bad roads and dilapidated culverts, mosquitoes and snakes, wild plants and bushes, and frequent natural calamities. And then he discovers that much of human misery comes from fellow human beings, if one can call them that. His attempts to change the system end in his violent death.

During one of his visits to the city, Shahed is taken by a friend, Asif, to Rebecca's posh house. On the way he had to pass by a couple of boys — a shoeblack and another who picks edibles from a dustbin (this was 1974). Rebecca's husband, Afzal, is engaged in export-import business, and, Asif suspects, in smuggling as well, which he does not mind because Afzal makes contribution to his party fund. Afzal is currently on a visit to Penang, Hongkong and Singapore, where he was rather unwilling to take along his wife, who understands that her presence will interfere with his pleasure. She is, however, not unhappy, because she has got other means of enjoyment. She shudders to think of the countryside where she was compelled to take refuge during the liberation war. Recollecting the condition of the toilets there, she exclaims that, it was better to have been raped by the invading army. Rebecca and Afzal represent a new set of people in Bangladesh who are closer to the corridors of power.

Shahed's death — and other acts of violence in the two novels — reflect on the state of human rights, but these are neither isolated nor novel incidents. Communal disturbances, fights over occupation of property, clashes among political workers, and such other happenings have been noted by the authors. The worst comes when the state or its agencies indulge in acts of violence. The most notable one was the shooting of people demanding the status of a state language for Bengali on 21 February 1952. It has left an indelible mark on our literature — the first example being the anthology,

Ekushe February (1953), edited by Hasan Hafizur Rahman. *Arek Falgun* (1969), a novel on the subject by Zahir Raihan (1935-72), ends with the promise: 'we shall return next February, twice in number'. And they have. Many times in the following years. One of the best novels of the kind is *Chilekothar Sepai* (1987) by Akhtaruzzaman Elias (1943-97), a chronicle of the mass upsurge of 1969 when the police and the army cut down many lives. The hero, Osman, an alienated young man, is confronted with so many deaths around him that he feels the compulsion of coming out of his shell, in violation of the curfew order. And the huge literature produced in Bangladesh on the war of liberation portrays the deplorable violation of human rights all over the country.

The coercion of the state machinery resulting in violation of human rights, has not, however, ended with the liberation of the country. To this has been added the phenomenon of *fatwa*—judgement handed down by the self-proclaimed custodians of public morality and religious principles—which has been directed mostly at women.

Our literature has reflected the situation obtaining at home over times. The writers have joined the people who can claim, in the words of Shamsur Rahman (b. 1927), the leading poet of Bangladesh:

The cataclysm has not put me to flight,
On my own plot of land, defiant
I've stood my ground, and this is
My kind of pride.

(Translated by Zillur Rahman Siddiqui)

MANY BHASHAS BUT ONE LITERATURE

U. R. Anantha Murthy

We have always lived in India in an ambience of languages. In the past Shankara who wrote in Sanskrit must have spoken Malayalam; and Madhwacharya in Udupi must have spoken Tulu and Kannda, but wrote in Sanskrit; and Ramanuja who must have been profoundly moved by the Alvar saints of Tamil also wrote in Sanskrit. Each of these great philosopher-saints, who propagated Advaita, Dvaita and Visishtavaita philosophies travelled through the whole country and had disciples all over India. They also influenced mystic poets in the regional languages of India through the centuries. Languages they spoke and the language they used for their learned discourse fulfilled specific functions in their lives. But the two did not remain apart. What was learned Philosophical speculation based on the Vedas became myth and poetry in the bhashas of the common people. Also, a profound egalitarian impulse entered into the hegemonic structure of the Indian society. The Dasas of Karnataka, Chaitanya of Bengal, the Alvars of Tamil are products of such a process within the tradition.

Something else also happened in India. Goutama Buddha didn't choose to write in Sanskrit. He questioned the authority of the Vedas and spoke the language of the unlearned masses. So too did the Jain philosophers. Later, in the medieval period (not the dark age as in Europe), the saint poets of India didn't use Sanskrit but the bhashas of India. They were mystics, their experience of God was immediate and not speculative. Basava, Tukaram, Kabir, Nanak and Chaitanya, by opting for the language of everyday speech for religious experience, empowered the languages of the masses. As a direct consequence of this option, their poetry empowered the women and people of low castes who spoke these languages. The spiritual insights and philosophical subtleties which marked Sanskrit, the language of the elite classes became thus the possession of the Indian bhashas. These bhashas, ever since the medieval period, have always been the conduits of egalitarian passion working through the history of India. It is a continuous process of inclusion, and no negation of any language, either of Sanskrit "the language of the Gods" in the past, or of Persian or English, "the languages of the powerful ruling classes" later on. The most recent of these great saints, who can be described as the critical insiders of Indian civilization, is Mahatma Gandhi, who wrote in Gujrati, Hindustani and also English.

In our times, what used to be the function of Sanskrit at one time for all India communication is taken over by English. Hence, the Indian Bhashas which had digested the essence of Sanskrit are at present coping with the challenges of the West. This is indeed no less a challenge than what the bhashas faced in relation to Sanskrit in a hierarchical society.

What was true of India in the past, therefore, seems to be more true today. We live in an ambiance of languages and of diverse influences wherever we may be living in India, particularly so if we live in one of the ubiquitous towns of India. One language at home, another on the streets, still another in the office of work — this seems quite usual and natural. If one has a mother at home who doesn't speak English and the daughter narrates to her what happened in the office, she has assumed the role of a translator unconsciously. We have always been such translators in the past as well.

A thousand years ago, Pampa, a great Jain poet in my language, Kannada wrote *Mahabharata* making Arjuna, his hero. Thus he idealized the Hindu king whom he served by comparing him to Arjuna. The Lord Krishna, who is the central figure for another great Hindu epic poet, Naranappa, could not have played the same divine function for Pampa in his recreation of the old epic, for Pampa was profoundly Jain in his faith. It is amazing how in the past one could work within a tradition and yet strike a new path to suit his religious faith. It is a transcription of the *Mahabharata*, which allowed him to remain true to his Jain faith, while expressing his worldly loyalty to the king of another faith. This is truly a memorable example of creative secularism in India's past, a thousand years ago.

Pampa's worldly concern does not end with mere official loyalty to the king. He uses his lively sense of his times to make an ancient epic to embody contemporary realities. Thus, in the poetic structuring of his work be manages to imbibe into the indigenous genius of his languages what Vyasa and Kalidasa could offer him in Sanskrit. He is still a model as a writer to contemporary poets in Kannada.

Not only transferring experiences of one language into another in a continuous and spontaneous act of translation in the course of our daily lives, we have also knit India together through the ages in Pampa's way. We have freely used Ramayana and Mahabharata for this purpose. Therefore, it is possible to say, that, apart from all the innumerable languages of India, there are two more languages, metaphorically speaking. These are the great epics, *Ramayana* and *Mahabharata*. Most of us, I would dare say, have not read these two epics for the first time, as a European can be said to have read his Homer.

I remember here what A.K. Ramanujan, a creative translator of Indian literature once narrated. He was collecting oral Ramayanas in the Kannada language. There are thousands of them. These folk *Ramayanas* are narrated from memory by the non-literate rural people. In one of these of *Ramayanas*, as in every one of them, Rama advises Sita that she should stay back in the palace and not accompany him to forest to which only he is exiled. Rama argues that Sita is a delicate princess and has never known suffering, and life in the forest is dangerous. Sita argues back that as his wife her dharma is to be by his side in joy and sorrow. The heated conversation is morally edifying to the listeners. What surprises is what follows. Rama comes up with very clever reasons for Sita to stay behind and serve his old and ailing mother. Then Sita demurs coyly, but firmly: "In every Ramayana that I know of, Sita goes to the forest with her husband. How can you then say no to me?" It is obvious that this rural Sita could not have read Valmiki, she needn't read him either. Like everyone else through the whole land, whatever be her mother-tongue, she inherits Valmiki's story. This is an excellent example for inter-textuality in Indian literary and cultural heritage. Thus we belong to pluralities of culture but to a single civilization.

Mathew Arnold, a great literary critic once wrote of what was required to make a complete reader of English literature. Along with a knowledge of his own literature, he should know another modern European literature, and the works of his ancestors in Greek and Latin languages. What we should note is that Arnold does not stop there but goes on to say that a knowledge of the Orient is necessary for a European writer, for the Orient is the "other" for him. The most creative of modern European writers Eliot or Yeats or Herman Hesse, have added something new to European view of life breaking new ground because of such an influence of the Orient on them.

For a modern Indian writer such a confluence of influences is not a result or deliberate seeking. It is there as a driving force of life in his immediate environment. A student who goes to a country college in Europe or United States of America could not have heard of Kalidasa or Valmiki. But a student in a mofussil college of India knows at least who Shakespeare is. There is more Europe in India, for historical reasons, than India in Europe.

Therefore for an Indian writer his situation in his culture is more complex and more challenging. We inherit not only our own ancient culture, but we have to deal with the rest of the world as a fact of unavoidable cultural influence. Besides, the bhashas in which the culturally rich masses have kept them alive. The elite in Indian society, whether in the past or globalising present, have been able to switch over to the language of the rulers of India; it was Persian once, and English now. They could choose the language of worldly advancement in their search for wealth and power but the common people who had no such choice have however survived and fortunately for us have preserved the languages of India, and their rich cultural memory in oral tradition. An illiterate woman in village may recite through her memory an epic. And this epic could be a great poem. The language of the poem may not even be listed in our Constitution; it is perhaps futile to hope that some day this language will be used for sophisticated and abstruse expository writing. Such a language may never have a Kant, but it can embody the vision of a Blake or the energy of a Homer. It keeps alive for us the primordial energies of a people close to nature without which no great poetry can be written.

An Indian writer, therefore, if he has to make a contribution in his language has to be related with equal intensity to his own classical past of his language, to the pan-Indian Sanskrit heritage, and to the inescapable western influence on him in actual socio-economic realities of his modern life. This is easily appreciated if one follows Arnold's prescription and suitably adapts it to Indian ethos. What needs to be added is often forgotten by our literary intellectuals. Perhaps more importantly and more immediately, the Indian writer is under profoundly aesthetic compulsion to recover for himself the richness of the texture of his language which has been nourished and kept alive in all its vitality in the everyday speech of the poor and the downtrodden of his land. This means a continuous fight against amnesia, and neglect of one's roots often brought about by empty and grandiose illusions of progress and development. The loss of sense of roots in one's soil is a danger inherent in the modern technological process of mindless globalization. the multi-layered structure of the Indian Bhashas may save us, hopefully, from such a loss of identity.

Before we became independent, something important happened in the history of the Indian Bhashas. We have had through the ages important writers in all the Indian languages. In Tamil, the oldest language perhaps after Sanskrit, there were even attempts to develop a poetics which can be seen as an alternative to the poetics in Sanskrit. And we had great writers like Tulsidas and Jnandev who became more than literary figures for the people who speak the languages in which they wrote. Yet, Kalidasa was the literary figure for Indian writers for a long time. A literary figure is not just a great writer. There are no greater writers for Indians than Valmiki and Vyasa. Yet Kalidasa was the literary figure, the figure to emulate in literary composition. Kalidasa also had the added advantage of being known through the whole country for he wrote in Sanskrit. He was pre-eminently a literary master. The only such literary figure who appeared in our times was Rabindranath Tagore. What is important here is that he wrote in one of the Indian bhashas and yet became a literary figure for emulation for all writers in India.

Tagore's success in one of the bhashas of India which is neither as ancient as Tamil, nor as widespread as Hindi is of great significance for our times in India. It means that any Indian bhasha has the potential to produce an all India literary figure. That we have many languages is not a handicap, but a blessing. Plurality of languages, cultures and religions has not in the past threatened the basic unity of our country. They have, on the other hand, contributed to the richness of the texture of our lives and allowed us to interact with one another. Moreover, the diversities while never threatening the unity of India, have, however, ensured the inevitability of democratic structure for our country. We are, as a consequence, not a nation-state in the narrow European sense, nor a homogenized 'big' nation like United States of America. We are primarily an ancient civilization, and the literature in or bhashas, with their history as well as their potential has contributed to our sense of a Nation with a difference.

THE RESILIENCE OF PAKISTAN'S PARALLEL THEATRE

Madeeha Gauhar

The sustained survival of Pakistan's Parallel Theatre for about 15 years, in spite of all the odds against it and all the predications of its demise, has surprised many, even some parallel theatre activities themselves. Eversince its modest and difficult beginning in early 80's, sceptic critics and cynical observers have been claiming that a theatre committed to social change and run by non-professional volunteers, is an aberration in a culturally hostile and aesthetically-barren society like Pakistan. But the parallel theatre has outlived General Zia-ul-Haq's military dictatorship and several quasi-democratic set ups and has shown no signs of withering away. In fact, if any, the sings are of steady though slow growth.

Pakistan has always been a rather unwelcoming place for art and culture, mainly because of the particular circumstances which led to the creation of Pakistan in 1947, as a result of the partition of India. Since the raison d'etre for the new state was the "two nation theory", the Pakistan Muslims had to prove that they were different from the Hindus. Any manifestations of common history or culture had to be forcefully rejected to prove the point. The continued hostility between independent India and the overwhelmingly Muslim Pakistan strengthened these attitudes and the Pakistani Establishment, using the threat posed by Indian hegemonic ambitions, found excuses for imposing authoritarian rule in the country as well as rejecting any expression of cultural or artistic activity which was common between the two countries. Classical dance, music, theatre, painting and sculpture were dubbed as Hindu culture, although the Muslims of the united India had great contributions of the development of these arts.

Not that Pakistanis did not inherit a rich and old civilization and did not enjoy dance and music or appreciate poetry and painting. In fact they are heirs to one of the oldest and most cultured civilizations in the world, the Indus Valley Civilization. The folk literature and arts, including folk theatre, had thrived in the past in areas now forming Pakistan. But the Muslims of Pakistan allowed, along with the departure of the Hindu and Sikhs, forcible expulsion of some of the most beautiful and valuable aspects of cultural heritage, just for the sake of temporary political objectives. The abnormal behaviour has cost Pakistan dearly, contributing to the break-up of Pakistan in 1971 and complicated ethnic, cultural and social problems.

The attitudes developed during the Pakistan Movement, were consolidated by the successive military dictatorship which found the India bogey a convenient ploy to maintain their grip on power. Hence the growth of art and culture was mostly suppressed or at best criminally ignored in the first 25 years of Pakistan. The Bhutto era (1972-77) was an exception to this rule. During this period, people's culture got a boost because of Zulfiqar Ali Bhutto's popular politics and progressive ideas. Various arts institutions were established such as the Academy of Letters, the Institute of Folk Heritage and the National Film Development Corporation. But just six years could not compensate for the loss of a quarter Century and Bhutto was soon deposed and hanged by a fundamentalist military chief.

Culture was General Zia-ul-Haq's first victim. One of the first things he did, apart from arresting all major political leaders, was the banning of Renowned Kathak dancer Naheed Siddiqui's dance programme on Pakistan Television "Payal". Psychological warfare expert General Mujib-er-Rehman was made the all-powerful head of the Information Ministry and Radio and Television. Any opposition to the military rule, even by gestures such as waving a V-sign, were made punishable by imprisonment and flogging. Many intellectuals and artists were among those arbitrarily arrested for demanding an elected civilian government. After terrorising the populace by the execution of Zulfiqar Ali Bhutto, further shock were inflicted on the people by the public hangings and floggings, massacres of workers and introduction of the so-called Islamic reforms. By 1983, benefitting from Murtaza Bhutto's ill-fated hijacking of a Pakistan International plane, the military regime had gagged Press, imprisoned political leaders and stopped all political activity.

This situation led to two kinds of reactions. One was the mushrooming and popularity of commercial theatre, which provided people with a chance to have a much-needed relief from the suffocating environment, even though the standards were abysmal. The second was the emergence of the parallel theatre. The commercial theatre, which was struggling to survive until then, become popular among economically-well off but culturally less aware classes, who were happy to pay for a good laugh and a dig or two at the system. They did not mind if the play was without a script or even without a director. The plays were usually bordering on vulgarity and bad taste but were also irreverent to authority. Interestingly a regime which was happy to flog people for waving victory sign under Martial Law, allowed the arts council and other halls to be used for such plays.

The parallel theatre activity started in Karachi and Lahore in early 1980s. It started with occasional productions inspired by committed individuals. The response was so encouraging that soon theatre groups like *Dastak* and *Tehrik-i-Niswan* in Karachi and *Ajoka* in Lahore were formed. As very few original scripts, appropriate for the situation, were available, the groups had to rely on adaptations. Some Indian scripts came in very handy, as they addressed relevant issues and were written in a similar milieu. Brecht became as popular as any Pakistani writer, as groups in Lahore, Karachi, Quetta and Hyderabad performed his plays. Later original plays started coming, though not as many as needed, and Pakistan's parallel theatre began developing.

The enthusiastic response which theatre groups received was partly because all other forms of dissent had been banned by the military regime and going to theatre become an act of definance and show of solidarity with the democratic movement. The parallel theatre audience included political, trade union and women activists, middle class theatre enthusiasts and students. The performers were mostly young amateurs, whose motivation was a mixture of defiance of dictatorship and desire for self-expression. Only a handful had some experience of theatre. But in those days the charged audience was more interested in radical content than in sophistication of production.

The parallel theatre showed admirable courage in the Martial Law days. They chose bold political and social themes and preferred to perform in open air or in make-shift ill-equipped halls rather than subject themselves to the governmental censorship. The plays such as *Ajoka's* "Barri" (about imprisoned women and Hudood Laws), *Tehirik-i-Niswan's* "Aurat" (about exploitation of women), *Lok Rehas'* "Andheray Da Pandh" (about oppressed classes and disillusioned youth), *Dastak's* "Galileo" (about the conflict between the seekers of truth and conservative Establishment) and *Sanjh's* "Bandiwan" (about the imprisonment and execution of a popular leader called "z") were scathing in their attacks on the fundamentalist dictatorial politics of General Zia-ul-Haq.

The parallel theatre plays in the 1980s were mostly issue-based and politically-motivated. Many groups opted to do street theatre and others were content with agit-prop theatre. The slogan-mongering and defiant political statements evoked enthusiastic response from the audience but some groups were not satisfied with that. They took upon themselves the task of laying the foundation of quality people's theatre, which focused on social and political issues but also presented an aesthetically satisfying and professionally sound theatre. *Ajoka* in Lahore and *Tehrik-i-Niswan* in Karachi strived to maintain this balance from their early days.

Though the parallel theatre got a lot of encouragement from the audience, the press and the community groups, this support did not translate into financial support. The theatre groups had to dig into their own or their friends' pockets to meet expenses in the earlier days. Gate money, wherever performances were ticketed, was barely enough to meet the expenses. This was in spite of the fact that the productions were almost always simple and cheap and almost everyone worked for free. In some cases NGOs or other political or social organizations paid for the expenses when they invited them for performances. But the movement survived.

With the end of the dictatorship, the new situation presented new challenges. On the one hand, there was more freedom of expression and the Arts Councils were now available, at least in principle, for the parallel theatre. But on the other hand, the theatre groups lost a lot of supporters who could now express themselves through permitted political activities. The initial euphoria however died down quickly when the groups discovered that through the freedom of political activities had been granted but social and economic problems remained as complex and grim as before. They also found that the Establishment's hostility towards parallel theatre still persisted. Much publicised activities such as the 'Pakistan National Council of Arts' national theatre festivals were done more for publicity than any serious intention to promote quality theatre. Arts institutions and government ministries did not take any serious steps to support parallel theatre or establishment institutions such as a National school of Drama or a Performing Arts Academy.

The parallel groups, realising that the revival of democracy had, not only opened few doors for them, it had also deprived them of an important reason for their existence, i.e., providing a rare forum for expression of dissent. They had to adjust according to the changed circumstances. Some like Karachi's *Dastak* and Lahore's *Sojhla* could not survive but others like *Ajoka*, *Lok Rehas* and *Tehrik-i-Niswan*, which had resisted the temptation of easy applause by resorting to slogan-mongering, did not find the readjustment that difficult. They had been picking social issues rather than specific political targets as themes of their plays and taking great care in pressing quality theatre. Hence they could carry on with their work without any interruption.

The parallel theatre, after the initial setback, recovered and resumed its work, playing the role of the social conscience of society, focusing on violations of human rights and exposing the forces of exploitation, discrimination and violence. In fact more groups were formed: *Naya Theatre* in Lahore, *Katha*, *Baang* and *Sevak* in Karachi and *Sanjh* in Islamabad. Groups have recently been set up in Peshawar, Hyderabad and Faisalabad. All these groups were formed by people already involved in or inspired by parallel theatre.

The thematic focus of the post-Zia parallel theatre has changed to a certain extent. The Zia period themes related to the Martial Law repression, execution of Z. A. Bhutto, fundamentalist policies against women and minorities and hypocrisy of the rulers. In the post-Zia period, the enemy is not as well-defined as the military dictator was, and the issues can no longer been seen in black and white. Now the themes are more focused on attitudes and issues in a long-term context. Recent plays have focused on issues such as environment, women's position in society and sectarian or ethnic violence.

The scale of Pakistan's parallel theatre, if compared with similar theatre movements in neighbouring countries such as India and Bangladesh, may be quite modest, but if evaluated in period of existence. Though only about a dozen groups are engaged in regular activity, they have established a tradition of serious quality theatre in the country. They have trained actors and theatre activists who have later moved on to perform on television or gone to other cities and set up new groups. The movement is now reaching wider audience through distribution of its videos and coverage of its work on television. In fact some of the groups have been able to produce and present their productions on television, without compromising on their content. *Ajoka* has presented its play on environment "Kali Ghata" on PTV and its popular comedy on family planning was adapted for PTV as a serial and became a hit. Earlier PTV's drama serial "Neelay Hath", based on *Ajoka's* play about imprisoned women and Hudood Laws, "Barri", had become very popular. *Tehrik-i-Niswan* produced long plays on feminist themes for PTV and the private network NTM. These productions have introduced the basic ideas of the parallel theatre to a very large number of Pakistani viewers. They have made some parallel theatre actors well-known, making it easier for them to attract audience when they perform at new places.

Through these TV productions, the parallel theatre groups have focused on some vital social issues in a manner which regular TV writers would be unable to do. In 1989, in drama serial "*Neelay*

Hath" (based on *Ajoka's* "*Barri*"), plight of women prisoners and victims of the anti-women Hudood Ordinance of Zia era was highlighted while women's right to education was the central theme of a *Tehrik-i-Nisawn* TV plays in 1994. Ajoka's play on family planning issues, "Jum Jum Jeevay Jammanpura" was adapted for a TV serial entitled "Janjalpura" (autumn 1996), which according to the Secretary Population planning "has done more for the promotion of family planning than any other initiatives".

At present, the parallel theatre faces two kinds of challenges for its survival and development. One is its relevance and attraction for the audience and the other is its financial viability. The theatre groups are still committed to producing plays on social issues but issues have become so complex and problems so compounded that a simplistic understanding and portrayal is unlikely to attract or inspire the audience. The political condition are hardly conducive either. There is no political party which is committed to human rights and social justice. Most of them are dominated by vested interest and ruling classes, having no interest in changing the status quo in favour of the people. People in general are fed up of political games being played by the major political parties and the activists are generally disillusioned. Trade unions have become weak and have lost influence; so much so that today the most effective trade union body is run by the fundamentalist Jammat-i-Islami.

The other challenge is posed by the proliferation of the TV channels, domestic and international, Now the viewers have a vast choice to choose from movies, music, sports or news channels, making it more difficult to persuade them to step out for theatre or any other cultural activity, especially if they have to pay for it as well.

The conservative sections of society are still hostile to performing arts, particularly those groups which have a liberal and modernistic approach. The Establishment is as insensitive and disinterested as ever. The cosmetic exercises of holding festivals or sending troupes are meaningless, and counter-productive in some cases. The PNCA's practice of sending third-rate productions to international festivals have angered the theatre groups and damaged Pakistan's cultural image. The Corporate sector is as uncultured as ever. It is very rare that an industrialist or a business concern would give even modest support to performing arts, especially theatre.

The financial viability of parallel theatre groups, therefore depends on two possible sources: (i) Financial assistance by NGOs or foreign donors for issues of mutual interest, and (ii) private productions for TV to gather funds which can be used for theatre.

The NGOs have become increasingly aware of the importance of theatre for mobilisation and awareness-raising. More and more NGOs working with the socio-economic problems of the people are inviting theatre groups for performances and training. NGOs which have sponsored or partially-funded parallel theatre productions include World Wide Fund for Nature (WWF), Family Planning Association of Pakistan, Human Rights Commission of Pakistan, Pakistan Medical Association, War Against Rape and Rotary Club of Pakistan. International donor agencies which have helped parallel theatre groups include Noraid, Dutch Embassy, ICCO, Global Fund for Women, Alliance Francaise and the Goethe Institute.

The Private productions for TV require heavy initial investment and the profit is not very high. However as new channels enter the field, the demand for privately-produced TV productions is bound to increase and experienced theatre groups are better placed to compete. But involvement with TV productions can also make the groups more involved in video productions and may eventually leave theatre altogether.

However as things stand today, the parallel theatre is still alive, if not kicking, and all predictions of its demise have proved to be premature. It has made its mark on the cultural map of Pakistan. Its themes and techniques have inspired many and set standards for those who enter the field. It has introduced talented and committed actors for theatre and TV. *Ajoka*, *Tehrik-i-Niswan*, *Punjab Lok Rehas*, *Naya Theatre* and Karachi Drama Circle have performed abroad and introduced Pakistani theatre at international level.

In a society which is in the grip of grave social, economic and political crisis, where moral deterioration has touched the lowest ebbs, where anarchy and chaos are running riot, survival of a theatre movement of committed volunteers, without any major sources of funds, is remarkable. The major factor for this phenomenon is the commitment and perseverance of the theatre activists. Another reason is the fact that the very crisis which has blocked parallel theatre's progress, has also created a desperate need for such theatre. People who do not find any hope in the real life and have lost faith in all leaders and ideologies, want some comfort, some catharsis and parallel theatre provides that. It attacks the status quo, it exposes the opportunist leadership and urges the audience to change. The issues raised in the plays are vital and urgent, the interaction between the actors and the audience is lively and exciting.

The resilience and the strength of the parallel theatre of Pakistan is one of the few positive things which have happened on the cultural scene. It is a source of hope for the forces of change and progress.

In the coming years, things are bound to become worse, both economically and socially and the times will become even more trying for the parallel theatre. Crisis at home and the challenge from across the borders and the skies are going to test this resilience to the fullest extent. It remains to be seen if the parallel theatre will be buried deep in the debris of the collapsing system or will survive to herald a renewal.

SOCIETY, THE STATE AND THE ARTIST: THE EVOLUTION OF CONTEMPORARY ART IN PAKISTAN

Naazish Ata-Ullah

The approach of almost a half century since Independence from the British provides us an opportunity to survey the spectrum of the visual arts in Pakistan with some degree of retrospection and insight. A complex, multi-layered canvas confronts us encompassing a myriad images, emotions, events and intellectual question. I will attempt to narrate and comment on these in this paper.

The nationalist movement in art which gathered impetus at the turn of the century in Bengal was a very significant attempt at rejecting the yolk of colonialism while striving to attain some form of a national identity in art. Whether the movement successfully achieved this objective or not is a debatable issue. However, in my view, the post-independence period has been in many ways a perpetuation of the earlier struggle and thus the last fifty years reveal that consciously and most certainly at the sub-conscious level the search for identity is a serious pre-occupation with the practitioners of the visual arts in Pakistan.

While we recognise that primarily the intrinsic concern of every artist is contained in achieving a balance between form and content, we also know that the artist's environment stimulates his or her creativity to respond, amongst other things, to the society of which the artist in an integral part. Based on this observation we can state that the artist holds a mirror to society and thus the establishing of a social and political role for the artist has also been a matter of general concern in our recent history. However, I must emphasise that juxtaposed against the natural concerns of the artists, we in Pakistan, have experienced the juxtaposed against the natural concerns of the artist, we in Pakistan, have experienced the strong arm of the State, especially during the course of three military take-overs — dictating, patronising, rejecting and interfering. Therefore we have to look at not only the process of making but also the way in which art has been received and directed in Pakistan.

I will focus more pointedly on the most recent twenty years of our history which bear grater relevance to the current discussion. However, the first three post-independence decades will also be discussed as they are imperative for a deeper understanding.

The euphoria which should have come in the wake of Independence was marred by the trauma of brutal violence which accompanied the mass migration across the borders of the new states of India and Pakistan. The re-settlement of refugees who additionally suffered an even greater psychological trauma, cast a state of unease, insecurity and confusion all over the country. Moreover, the untimely death of the top leadership — both the Quaid-e-Azam Muhammed Ali Jinnah and Liaquat Ali Khan — added to the general chaos. The scenario in the arts was equally dismal in the city of Lahore which was, as it is today, the cultural capital of the western region, similar to Calcutta in the east. At Independence it was the centre of all forms of educational and cultural activity. A number of libraries, universities, colleges, two open-air theatres and at least twelve other theatres were located in Lahore. It was the centre of the film industry prior to Bombay and many stars including Noorjehan, Kamini Kaushal, Dev Anand, Dilip Kumar and Mohammed Rafi had worked there before Independence. Moreover the premier institutions of art production, the Mayo School of Arts and the Department of Fine Art of Punjab University were also located there.

Independence brought confusion to most institutions in Lahore including its art schools and studios. The valuable archives of the Mayo School of Art were destroyed including its records, books and the works of its illustrious students; some of its ustads migrated to

India. In an interview, the late Anna Molka Ahmed, former Head of the Fine Art Department at the Punjab University remarked: "immediately after Independence we were left without our teachers and most of our student body and we had to start from scratch". Division of assets between Pakistan and India resulted in the division of the famous collection of the Central Museum in Lahore between Lahore and Chandigadh, source of cultural activity in the city, was locked and subsequently abandoned after it had been looted. Only a few of his sculptures were rescued to be later ensconced in the Lahore Museum. I am referring deliberately to these events in the early years of Pakistan to emphasise the period of chaos and upheaval which necessitated return to order and the need to progress by way of defining new directions. Thus, the first decade of Pakistan is one in which new directions were given to the arts. I may bring to your notice that in these early years Abdul Rahman Chughtai and Ustad Allah Bakhsh in the west and Zainul Abedin in what is now Bangladesh were the most imposing figures on the art scene.

The Mayo School of Art, established in 1875, was primarily a professional school of design with a small department of fine art. It also ran a course for the training of architectural draughtsmen. By contrast the University of the Punjab's Department of Fine Art, although smaller in size, was more academic in its approach and concerned to a lesser degree in the training of professional practitioners. During the fifties, an era when the foundations of an industrial base for Pakistan were being laid, the Mayo School which was administered by the Department of Industries, was an ideal training ground for professionals required to meet the challenges of the newly emerging market. It was therefore decided in 1958 to up-grade the institution to a professional college level, to rename it the National College of Art, and to create three full-fledged departments of design, architecture and fine art. At this stage both Sheikh Ahmed and Shakir Ali, eminent painters, were on the faculty of the School. While the search was on for a suitable principal to head the institution, an American, professor Mark Sponenburgh, was selected and appointed from London. Two years earlier a Mr. Sidney Spedding, an English sculptor, had also been employed as principal of the School. The point to emphasise is that the bureaucrats, victims of a 'past-colonial state of mind', preferred to employ one foreigner after another despite the presence of two very competent and respected Pakistani professionals. Consequently, a frustrated Sheikh Ahmed resigned and Shakir Ali, a more genial man, worked under Sponenburgh later succeeding him as Principal in 1963.

Meanwhile NCA graduates began to make their presence felt in the market and fulfilled the market demand with remarkable competence. Both men and women from the College could be found in advertising agencies, in television as designers, in textile mills, ceramic factories, the government printing press etc. Qualified architects were also absorbed in the market and the fine artists set about establishing a reputation both nationally and internationally under the guidance and inspiration provided by Shakir Ali.

Although Chughtai and Allah Bakhsh were the most celebrated and successful artists in the fifties, it was their contemporary Shakir who pioneered the modern movement in Pakistani art. Shakir was trained in the European manner but his work resonated influences from his own visual tradition. Simplicity of line and form and a strong presence of colour dominated his paintings rendering them contemporary with a wider universal appeal. His images were inspired by a sensitivity to his own environment making the Bengal School sentimentality and nostalgia for the past in Chughtai and Ustad Allah Bakhsh's paintings obsolete. Unlike them there was no yearning for the past in his work; instead, while still mindful of his tradition, there was a celebration of the present. In the late fifties in Lahore an energetic and serious group of painters were working on similar themes, discussing intellectual issues and holding exhibitions. The group included the painters Safdar, Moyene Najmi, Hanif Ramay, Shemza, Ahmed Pervez, and Ali Imam. Many performing artists and writers including Imtiaz Ali Taj and Faiz Ahmed Faiz, together with the painters and including Shakir Ali and Khalid Iqbal, met on a regular basis to discuss issues of mutual concern. Organised into a private body called the Lahore Arts Council they had their studios and a theatre on the premises of the current Alhamra Arts Complex in Lahore. Over a period of time and through constant State machinations the independent status of the

Lahore Arts Council was forced to be taken over completely by the State thereby causing a complete transformation in its original form. Although an imposing structure, designed by the architect Neyyar Ali Dada, was constructed under the Martial Law Governor Jilani in Zia-ul-Haq's regime, State interference to the extent of banning of exhibitions, dance performances and staging of plays to the censorship of the same occurred which resulted in its boycott by many artists and performers. Also in more recent times the Alhamra Arts Complex has been used as a convention centre by whichever political party is in power.

Amongst some of the earliest attempts to visually explore an ideological identity, I refer back to painters from the Lahore Arts Council group who undertook experimentation into a contemporary rendition of calligraphy, traditionally considered to be the highest form of Islamic art. These explorations were purely motivated by aesthetic concerns unlike the later abuse of calligraphy which was promoted as 'modern' Pakistani art. Shakir's mural for the Punjab Public Library is an excellent example of this such as are the earlier works of Hanif Ramay, Shemza and Sadequain. But, it was Sadequain who became the torch-bearer for a phase of 'modern' calligraphic painting: a means of expression which began within the aesthetic domain but steadily deteriorated as it gained State patronage.

In 1957, Sadequain's first exhibition was opened by Prime Minister Hussain Shaheed Suhrawardy who personally promoted the talented young artist. He was sent to work in Paris where his paintings were greatly appreciated winning him a commission to illustrate Camus. Sadequain's Parisian sojourn culminated in a series of figurative paintings strongly inspired by traditional calligraphy. Strong, dark and angular forms loomed against the landscape in these works which I believe are amongst the best of Sadequain. When he returned, Pakistan was under its first military dictatorship and he became the most favoured of all artists of the Ayub Khan regime. He was commissioned to paint a mural for the new State Bank of Pakistan building in Karachi and a huge mural in the power-house building of Mangla Dam. On the basis of his calligraphy, many other state commissions followed including ones for Karachi Airport and for the Lahore Museum. His earlier work was mostly in a strong narrative mode reminiscent of the Latin American painters but his concern with calligraphy which persisted throughout his life sadly led to a gradual deterioration in his later work. These paintings were of no great artistic merit only a marble and Perspex but significantly they became synonymous with State sponsored 'official art'. A similar situation prevailed in the realm of architecture. Pakistan is full of examples of architecture from the Raj period. Although we are severely critical of the British for transformations they caused in our indigenous tradition we must accept that in most cases they evolved an architecture which was more sensitive to the local climate and in some cases even to existing forms than most architecture produced in the post-colonial era. Some of the most appalling examples of architecture have mushroomed all over the country — many under state sponsorship. In the sixties, state-sponsorship was also extended to architects from abroad in the planning and development of the new capital Islamabad. There an imperialist style adorns the buildings of government which is totally alien both to Pakistani visual culture and to the surrounding landscape. To further confound the vision and interspersed between the concrete and the foliage (the city's only saving grace) are the 'Islamisized' versions of architecture — a poor pastiche of a universally acknowledged great tradition. These buildings are again the outcome of state direction and can best be labelled 'Islamic kitch'. Such buildings are visible in every major city in Pakistan and are invariably financed by the State.

While summing up he first two decades of Pakistan we observe that there was not only a need to build new institutions but also a desire to find new directions which would reflect a national identity. The rise of individual artists such as Gulgee, Shakir Ali and Sadequain occurred in the absence of an explicit policy for the promotion of the arts. Hence the production of art was limited and it produced no definite social impact. A degree of state patronage was therefore extended to work which was perceived as representing a national identity whether it was found in the visual narratives created by Sadequain in his murals, or in the depiction of calligraphy which was also perceived as a symbol of Islamic identity.

State patronage and its active involvement in concrete terms was evident in the democratic period under Zulfiqar Ali Bhutto (1972-1977). There was a resurgence of cultural complex was envisioned in the capital Islamabad with branches in the regional centres. Many institutions for the promotion of culture were established. These included NAFDEC the institute for film and drama, the PIA dance academy, the Lok Virsa, Music Research Cell, National Book Foundation, the National Puppet Theatre, the Academy of Letters and a body called the Pakistan National Council of the Arts for music, literature and the visual arts which had the poet Faiz Ahmed Faiz as its first Director General. Plans were also drawn up for a National Gallery which is currently under construction after two decades. In the field of art education, the National college of Arts was taken over by the Federal Ministry of Education and its staff and students were involved in major cultural projects. Zahoor-ul-Akhlaq designed a monument for the National Sports Complex in Islamabad and the College participated actively in a mass gymnastic display.

Not only did the State extend support to all the arts but also, in line with its populist rhetoric, attempted to bring art to the masses. The newly created institutions in particular were called upon to devise programmes to implement this policy. A number of artists responded to the new wave such as Ijaz-ul-Hasan, Bashir Mirza and younger painters. Due to the imposition of martial law in 1977 this period was short-lived. The end of democracy crippled most of these institutions rendering them ineffectual and a mockery of the original. All progressive and creative persons concerned with these institutions were replaced. Many artists perceived as 'leftist' were marginalised whilst many other 'conformists' profited.

Of the periods of military rule in Pakistan, Zia-ul-Haq's dictatorship (1977-1988) was the most oppressive for the arts. The process of 'Islamisation' meant direct State interference which resulted in the promotion and projection of artistically the most mundane and banal and the total lack of support for the most creative and dynamic work. The State's policies promoted calligraphy as the politically acceptable 'Islamic' art form and a burgeoning of the most ill-conceived and superficial examples of painting and sculpture such work extended to embassies abroad and even artists like Sadequain and Gulgee jumped onto the 'official' bandwagon compromising their critical faculties by a proliferation of the most profane examples of 'Islamic art.'

On this despondent note I would like to turn to the alternative art scene during Zia's dictatorship and the consequent development of the art scene generally. Prime Minister Bhutto was hanged in the month of April while preparation for the NCA's degree show was in progress. The group of final year students responded in violent protest with painting depicting flesh, blood, hanged bodies, bolts and locks. Some professional artists reacted in a similar manner. Oppression produced its own reaction amongst artists both young old. As the external environment appeared to be hostile to freedom of expression there followed many years of internalisation where a lot of work was executed with vigour, determination and social awareness. Most importantly a process of politicisation occurred amongst the artist community which resulted in a very dynamic and socially conscious output. Some of the most sophisticated paintings were produced in Pakistan during the eighties, in times when the State was actively interfering in the arts by the imposition of rules and regulations which were designed to curb the freedom of expression. The forces of obscanturism prevailed time and again beginning with the ransacking of Colin David's exhibition, held in his house, by members of the Jamiat-i-Tulaba. Iqbal Hussain's paintings of Hira Mandi (the 'red light' area in Lahore) were not allowed to be shown at the Alhamra Arts Complex in Lahore as they promoted "vulgarity" and Salima Hashmi's work was taken down from the National Exhibition in 1979 as its content was 'political'. Jamal Shah's sculptures were also removed from an exhibition in Lahore as 'sculpture' was deemed un-Islamic. Representatives of the Jamiat-i-Tulaba forced their way into the National College of Arts and smashed a 100 years old wooden screen in the Principal's office and the College was threatened with closure if the works of its students showed 'nudity'. The reaction to the forces of the state evoked a greater resolve to protest by the artist community which responded by depicting in its works the brutality and intolerance that had pervaded the society. Notable amongst artists of this genre are the painters Nagori, Quddus Mirza, Anwar Saeed and a host of women. Some of these painters chose a direct means of depiction whereas others were more indirect in their approach choosing the use of symbols and metaphors to communicate their ideas. This manner of painting not only enhanced their personal visual vocabulary but it also contributed positively to the general development of the medium in exciting new ways. These years created an environment where some artists such as Zahoor-ul-Akhlaq emerged with a remarkable synthesis of the traditional with the modern and this manner of intellectualism in painting also entered the domain of architecture in the work of Kamil Khan Mumtaz.

Although there has been an increasing number of artists responding to the social and political environment since the 1980s it is the women artists who have emerged as the most significant force from this period — undaunted and powerful. Challenging the Law of Evidence imposed by Zia-ul-Haq, the fledgling Women's Action Forum took out a demonstration on the Mall Road, Lahore in 1983, which was broken up by a violent lathi-charge. This was a turning point in the politicising of women generally and in the arts in particular — a position from which there has been a steady growth. Women artists have not only responded to oppressive laws and to human rights abuses through their work but have also played a leading role in the feminist struggle along with other women's organisations. I would like to show the work of a selected few to illustrate my point.

To conclude it can be said that the political and social awakening of the Bhutto years reached a turning point during the repressive decade under Zia-ul-Haq. In response, there was a distinct politicisation of the artist. The most socially relevant work was began during this era and there has been no turning back since. The artist today is seriously concerned with the role and the relevance of his/her work in society.

THE TWO EXTREMES OF PERFORMING ARTS IN PAKISTAN

Sarwat Ali

The Dramatic Art in Pakistan have made steady progress over the years despite considerable pressures in the shape of censorship policies of the government and hostile reactions from a sizeable body of citizens who view the performing arts as contrary to the tenets of their faith.

Broadly speaking the dramatic arts can be divided into two categories. One that only aims to provide entertainment and the other that has an alternative vision of looking at contemporary situation. This may be too simple a categorization but it is sufficient to understand the two extremes as within these two extremes of instruction and pleasure falls the entire body of dramatic work.

In the first category falls the entire film industry of the country. A few films have been made with the honest intention of bringing in an element of the "serious" into the cinema but these have been so few and far between, and so unsuccessful with the ordinary film goer that its mere mention serves no other purpose than to bring it on record. The great bulk of the films have been made with the express intention of providing entertainment and hence appealing to populist aesthetics.

But despite wholesale condemnation the themes and characters that have given pleasure to the ordinary cine goer have changed in the last forty years or so. The earlier films mostly revolved round family issues, the most problematic and attractive being that of marriage, and marriage brought with it romance and repressed erotica. It was reflective of the primary issue of sex as in a segregated society, and one dominated by the primacy of the family rather than the individuality of personal love, this problem had been treated with broad and finer strokes by nearly all the film makers — and they got an audience for it in most cases. And in most cases the resolution of the film is in these extremes coming together thus bridging the wide chasm and apparently insurmountable polarity. The two families that initially had disapproved of the individuality of love become more appreciative of their emotional honesty by agreeing to give it the sanction of a socially acceptable institution — marriage.

The resolution of any problem including the central problem of love is arrived through a consensus. Since cinema is the medium with nearly the largest outreach most of the film makers do not consider it safe to strike any mean which upsets the prevalent order in society. Most of the films may be quite outrageous in the first half but are watered down considerably in the second one so as to remove any doubts or misunderstanding about the final message that it delivers. This compromise in the end is totally in favour of a broad populistic understanding of the basic rules and norms that has always controlled cinema in this country. But marriage and repressed erotica has been set aside by the other dominant trend based on violence. This violence too is not undefined or left to the audience's imagination but is stated as the direct result of some tangible injustice. In such films it is the force of revenge that shapes any logic in an order that otherwise has fallen prey to the rule of the jungle — avarice and the domination of the might against constitution of this lawless land, and it is through more violence that some semblance of honour is restored. In view of the collapse of the normal institutions the only way out remains the vindication of personal honour. The overall scenario is that of private justice and fall back upon the valour and courage of an individual — a hero.

The popular cinema has not risen above the issue of marriage and the cult of the individual hero. Perhaps it mirrors the structures that are very much relevant in this society but are pushed under the carpet or into blind spots by a small minority of people who want to see this society otherwise. The trends which have dominated cinema have now also seeped into the theatre as well. The theatre too can divided into the two categories mentioned earlier in the paper. But these two categories have enough meat to support it contrary to the films where the serious aspect is missing altogether or is so small as to be of no consequence.

Commercial theatre has become popular in the last twenty five years or so. From its humble beginnings in the late nineteen sixties it has grown at an accelerated rate. The fact that Lahore can boast of at least three private theatre halls — two of which have been converted from cinema halls is enough testimony to the fact that theatre has become a viable proposition.

On the average six plays are staged every day in Lahore — a city which happens to be the centre of both film and theatre in the country. The plays are usually very loosely constructed with ample scope and provision for ad libbing and double entered. The audience too respond to the improvisational pieces much more than the actual script. Though it might sound simplistic but this trend in theatre started because of the severe censorship policies of the various governments over the last forty years. Since the scripts were totally ripped apart by the censors, which comprised of personnel either from the administrative side of the government or from the Information Departments there was not enough left for the actors to perform. The actual meat was taken away from the scripts.

The actors then moved in by filling up this skeleton by ad libbing. What the censors had passed eventually turns out to be quite different when performed on stage. So big and heavy become the reliance on ad libbing that the entire emphasis shifts to the actor to become his theatre. The other aspects of the theatre like script, direction, set design, lighting and costume became much less important and absolutely secondary.

The ad libbing made two admissions — political satire came in as well as sexual innuendos. Sex too has been a taboo both in society and more so in show business but ironically and as it happens it finds other ways, not always very healthy and straight, to express itself. In the end both in our films and theatre there is a very strong undercurrent of sexuality which keeps erupting every now and then in its own perverted form.

There has always been paucity of scripts and nearly a total blackout where good scripts are concerned. In the beginning — in those innocent days usually western drawing room comedies were adapted and staged. It probably came into the mainstream theatre through such adaptations done at the theatre clubs of the colleges, mainly Government College at Lahore. As theatre grew in popularity and scale these drawing room comedies gradually were adapted on a larger extent and indigenized. The initial adaptations may now appear like translations as these adaptation are now so heavily worked upon that they only retain a very tenuous bond with the original work.

Scripts are still a problem with theatre, the same old scripts, adaptations of drawing room comedies are staged, though heavily worked upon, and these scripts are being repeated over and over again and not necessarily under the same title. The same script may have been staged under different title and names in the last thirty years or so. Of course this is facilitated by the fact that the script is only peg for the actors to hang their improvisational nuggets on. And these actors usually performing as stand up comedians and acting as in a one man show have honed their skills to perfection. Take these improvisational wizards away and nothing remains of the play. These actors therefore charge the highest sum because the entire play, so to speak, is dependent upon their performance.

Some of the plays have been in the same manner directly political but in much and many more cases the political satire is in the shape of a wisecrack or an outlandish remark. Most of the humour is statemental and often topical and reference fly off the actors lines in abundance. These plays have also more than reflected the main trends and currents in society. For example the exodus of Pakistanis to the Middle East resulted in a sudden change in the social balance of classes. This become an endemic theme — other than this the prowling liberalization especially of women is a perennial source and stoke for comedy — as is the rise to political power of people who have made their fortunes through illegal means. The state machinery like the working of the police too has been a stock theme with theatre and show business.

The people who watch this kind of theatre fall in a higher economic bracket than the ones who patronize the cinema. The rate of ticket in the theatre ranges from fifty to one hundred and twenty rupees which makes it two to four times more expensive than the films. This type of theatre of course has spread on to other cities of the Punjab. Theatre and plays are frequently held in cities like Faisalabad and Gujranwala by the same team of performers who have made theatre such a roaring business in Lahore.

In the last twelve years a parallel movement in theatre has also made its presence felt alongwith the boom of commercial theatre. Since these plays were constructed round themes which were more political these came directly under the preview of the strict censorship policies that were ruthlessly imposed during the martial law regime. The content of these plays revolved round repressive steps taken in various phases of life perpetrated as a consequence of the consolidation of martial law years.

Since the regimes found great fault with these plays permissions were withheld to stage these at public places and proper theatre halls constructed for this purpose. These plays initially were staged in the back lawns of private houses and then found refuge in some of the foreign cultural missions at Lahore and Karachi.

Dastak the first group to start this theatre of defiance in Karachi was soon followed by *Ajoka* in Lahore. Other groups then stepped in to do a number of plays again in the back lawns of private houses and foreign cultural missions. The more famous among these groups have been Lok Rehas, Naya Theatre and Saanj in Lahore and Tehrik e Niswan, Gripps Theatre and Creative Workshop in Karachi.

The two most famous plays of Dastak have been adaptations of Bretcht's *Exception and the Rule* and *Galileo* in which the issues of freedom of thought and action had been raised while the most outstanding plays presented by *Ajoka* have been a mixture of adaptations and original plays. The list is long and impressive — *Julous* was about freedom of political action, *Bari* was about the oppressive custom of dowry, it was about bonded labour, *Jhalli kithey jaway* was about the tradition of labelling and condemning women with independent minds, *Chula* on domestic violence, *Lappar* on discrimination on the bases of sex, alongwith the adaptations of *Three Penny Opera, Causasian Chalk Circle, Good Person of Scechaan*, all classics and too well known to be repeated here.

Since the end of the Martial Law regime and ushering in of a democratic era these groups have diversified on the themes of their plays. Now thematically these plays are built round issues which are very much a part of our social and political practice but are extremely retrogressive in character to inhibit the creative growth of this society. The question of the changing roles of women in society has been a major concern with the groups like *Ajoka*, *Lok Rehas* and *Tehrik e Niswan* while the rise of fundamentalist forces, and the discrimination on the basis of religion and sex and the environmental and problems of population are themes shared by most.

These groups have also staged adapted or dramatized short stories. The short story has been a very vibrant and potent form of expression which was given a new lease of life with the input of realism as a result of the influence of the Progressive Writers Movement in the thirties and then later in the fifties. These stories written by some of the biggest names in Urdu fiction like Manto have also dealt realistically with issues that have bedeviled ordinary men in their daily lives. Both *Ajoka* and Creative Workshop have particularly been active in staging plays on the short stories of Manto.

The proliferation of theatre has also resulted in the Lahore Arts Council liberalizing its policies as all those groups which were forbidden from using the premises and facilities have now been allowed to use its facilities. The parallel theatre is no longer on the fringe — it has become mainstream theatre if a distinction can still be maintained between mainstream and commercial theatre.

The Lahore Arts Council has done its own productions in the last five years and some of their plays have been considered the classics of Urdu drama like *Raa o Niaz*.

The electronic media in the country has been under state control. Pakistan Television Corporation was established more than thirty years ago as an autonomous body under the Ministry of Information. About seven years ago another channel was set up where besides relays of CNN private productions are televised. Initially it functioned independently but gradually over the years the government members have formed a majority in the Board of Governors that run this television network.

Despite rigid state control television plays have not really been towing an orthodox line in strict compliance with the directives of the government. Television was set up under a quasi military regime to propagate the views of the government in control but the creative aspect soon began to take the major portion of its prime viewing time as the teleplays became the most sought after programme on television.

Television has been used for blatant propaganda by all the regimes. Its News coverage has always been extremely partial and one sided, the discussion shows are all meant to authenticate the action of the government, its documentaries are made to verify the great advancement that the country has made under the policies of the government but the plays have often been more independent, closer to life and loaded with meaning which spills over one dimensional propaganda. During the martial law years teleplays also came under strict control of the government and most were dished out to legitimize the proceeding of the government. The overwhelming number justified certain religious injunctions in tandem with the government's line to establish its repressive and unrepresentative nature through the tendentious exploitation of certain tenets of religions. Some of the leading writers in sympathy with the policies of the government lend whole hearted support to these proceedings. In the plays of Ashfaq Ahmed for example the emphasis of any resolution especially of social conflict was seen as a consequence of fate. Fatalism was being preached unashamedly by the leading ideologue of the regime and in the face of evil resigned words of wisdom which more or less pointed to the maintenance of status quo were preached. He would select themes like advancement and equate it with avarice and greed, he picked on the exploitation of women and advised them to stay at home and not venture out to seek their own destiny. His wife Bano Qudsia too actively upheld the subordinate role that women should play to preserve the prevalent order.

But now the rigid control has been unloosed and there is greater freedom but at the same time, realism which was the strongest point of our television plays is being gradually replaced by a more tinsel presentation. Television now has much more glamour and affection that it did in the years when it was in the process of establishing itself.

There is much that can be shared by the people connected with the Dramatic Arts in South Asia because of a common pool of experience in this respect.

An annual festivals of Film and Theatre should be held in which groups from South Asia should participate. Seminars should be held on the problems faced by the Dramatic Arts within the South Asian context.

LITERATURE AND THE THEATRE IN CONTEMPORARY SRI LANKA

K. N. O. Dharmadasa

Introduction

Contemporary Sri Lanka has a trilingual literary tradition, that is to say there is literary activity in Sinhala as well as in Tamil and English. It is in Sinhala, the language of the largest ethnic/linguistic group that we naturally find the numerically largest contribution in literary activity. The majority[1] of the novels and short stories, collections of poems, plays and films produced and the largest number of newspapers and periodicals published are in Sinhala. To give some figures, there are three national dailies, and four week-end papers in Sinhala while there are two Tamil dailies and two week-end papers. We have two English dailies and four week-end papers. In addition, there are a large number of weekly and monthly publications in Sinhala, far outnumbering similar publications in the other two languages. In book production too the picture is similar.

In the present study the major focus will be on works in Sinhala. There will also be reference to works in Tamil and English as occasion demands.

Sinhalese, an Indo-European language has a rich literary tradition going as far back on the 3rd century BC. Classical Sinhala literature is largely a Buddhist literature heavily influenced by Pali and

---

[1] According to the last census (1981) Sinhalese comprise 74% of the population while there are 18.2% Tamils and 7% Sri Lankan Moors. The larger portion of the SL Moors have Tamil as their mother-tongue.

Sanskrit models. The compendiums of stories, the story poems, the message poems (*sandesa*), didactic verse and exegetical works, which form part of a long established classical tradition, are suffused by a heavy Buddhist atmosphere. At the same time however, the influence of classical Sanskrit poetry of the *Alankaravaadii* tradition is also seen in the Sinhala story poems and the *sandesa.*

With the advent of western powers to the island, the Portuguese, the Dutch and the English, from the early 16th century and the final subjection to the British empire in 1815, Sinhala literature came to be influenced by the culture and literature of the west. The first notable aspect of western culture that influenced Sinhala literature was Christianity. While a Sinhala Christian literature appeared on a small scale in the 17th century a more widespread western influence was to emerge only after the British subjugation of the whole island in 1815. The modernization of Sinhala literature began during the second half of the 19th century. The processes of modernization continued during the 20th century with the coming of newspapers and periodicals, the introduction of the novel and the short story and the emergence of an urban theatre and the spread of English education.

The first phase of modern Sinhala literature during the late 19th and early 20th centuries was characterized by a deep involvement in religious controversy. Firstly, the Christians used newspapers and the periodicals, fictional writings and the theatre for purposes of proselytism and this provoked the Buddhists to turn to the same means to defend their religion. The most prolific novelist of the early modern period, Piyadasa Sirisena (1875-1946) used the genre to criticize westernization and to uphold the virtues of the Sinhala-Buddhist culture. C. Don Bastian (1852-1921) and John De Silva (1852-1922), the foremost dramatists of the late 19th and early 20th centuries, produced a large number of plays glorifying the ancient Sinhala civilization. Sirisena, Bastian and De Silva are also the principal representatives of a revivalist era in which literature and the theatre were utilized for an ideological purpose — that of upholding traditional culture against the trends of westernization.[2]

[2] For details see K N O Dharmadasa *"Language, Religion and Ethnic Assertiveness: The growth of Sinhalese Nationalism in Sri Lanka"*, Ann Arbor, The University of Michigan Press, 1992, pp. 126-29.

With Sirisena, Bastian and De Silva we see the early emergence of a social consciousness among the Sinhala literati, and the emergence of an opposition to westernization, which they believed was deleterious to the national interest. They utilized their writings to resist this trend. Viewed from the point of view of secularism and communalism, these works may appear as sectarian and retrogressive. A more sympathetic view of the role they were playing might emerge if we place their works in the socio-cultural context in which they appeared. For example, in the *Sinhala Paraabhava Naatakaya* (a drama on the degradation of the Sinhalese) 1902, De Silva depicted the story of an Anglicized family, which like the proverbial deer run after chimeras before finally succumbing to a tragic end. The head of the household over-extends himself to keep up with luxuries of westernization, resorts to cheating and ends in prison. Addressing the audience he exhorts them draw the appropriate moral from his misfortune:

> To imitate a foreign life
> Is a path full of error
> See its dangers clearly
> And learn from my misfortune[3]

We find similar depictions of the tragic consequences of the Sinhalese trying to imitate the westerners in most of Piyadasa Sirisena's novels. It needs mention here that both Sirisena and De Silva were at the forefront of the powerful temperance movement which emerged at the turn of the century. As seen by Anagarika Dharmapala (1846-1933) the foremost champion of the Sinhala-Buddhist cause in early 20th century Sri Lanka.[4] It was:

> "our welfare-loving" and "just in all respects" Englishman who paved the way for drunkenness among the Sinhalese people ... The more the drinking of *toddy* and *arrack* increases, to the same degree the Sinhala race will go on the path of decline ... The Sinhala man, having sold his land, drinks toddy and arrack, becomes a slave to the white man and toils for him. (*Sinhala Bauddhaya*, 3 February 1912)

---

[3] See Sarath Amunugama "John De Silva and the Sinhala Nationalist Theatre" in *Ceylon Historical Journal*, 25, nos. 1-4, pp 285-304.

[4] Kumari Jayawardene, "Economic and political Factors for the 1915 Riots" *Journal of Asian Studies*, Volume XXIX (2), 1970, pp.223-34.

The revivalists were, not merely anti-colonial or anti-imperial: they were anti-alien as well. In the words of Dharmapala:

> "The island of Lanka belongs to the Sinhalese. For 2455 years this was the land of birth for the Sinhalese people. Other races have come here to pursue their commercial activities. For the Europeans, apart from this land there is Canada, Australia, South Africa, England and America to go; for the Tamils there is South India; for the Moors ... Egypt; the Dutch can go to Holland. But for the Sinhalese there is only this island." (*Sinhala Bauddhaya*, 20 January 1912)

Such "anti-alien" attitudes were the result of a growing fear among the urban Sinhala populace in particular, that they would be overwhelmed by the influx of foreigners, European, Indian and others, in the city of Colombo, and its suburbs. The Sinhalese traders felt threatened by European, Moor and Tamil traders and the Sinhalese working class was feeling insecure as a result of the large influx of Tamil and Kerala workers who were often prepared to work more for much less[4] than their Sinhalese counterparts and rivals.

While the major literary figures of the day were overtly communalistic in their responses to these issues, there were also the beginnings of a more socially conscious response to the plight of the poor and the down-trodden in urban centres, and a deep concern for social justice. An early instance of this is seen in they story Kuveni Hami in *Gahaniyak* (1925) the first collection of short stories by Martin Wickramasinghe (1891-1976).

Kuveni Hami, a girl from a poor family, who becomes a domestic servant in a Colombo mansion is seduced by a young master of the household. Thrown out, she drifts to a slum in the city and becomes the mistress of the labourer from Kerala, a drunkard. Unable to bear his constant harassments she attacks him with a knife and kills him. Brought before the court of law her fate is decided upon by the judge who happens to be the man who had molested her years ago. Apart from its biting criticism of the urban upper class, this story contains a vivid portrayal of the squalor in the slums of Colombo. The author has also been able to draw our attention to the hopeless situation of the poor and ignorant women of the lower strata of society who are exploited physically as well as sexually.

Kuveni Hami was unusual in the Sinhala fiction of that time. From their early appearance during late 19th century, Sinhalese fictional works were mainly propagandist. At a later stage we find romance emerging as the major concern. The works of A Simon De Silva (1874-1920) were mainly romances although a strong influence of Buddhist revivalism is also discernible in them. With W A Silva (1892-1957) who became the most popular novelist and short story writer, of the second and third decades of the twentieth century, we find a complete adoption of the popular pot-boilers in the vein of English writers such as Hall Caine and Rider Haggard.[5]

The Novel as Political Tract

With Martin Wickramasinghe's *Gamperaliya* ("The Changing Village", 1944) we see the beginnings of a strong social concern in fiction writing. *Gamperaliya* depicted the disintegration of traditional village life under the impact of modernization. It was followed by *Yuganthaya* (1948) and *Kali Yugaya* (1957) where the depiction of social transformation was continued, narrating the story of the rise of the bourgeoisie with its urban base and entrepreneurial drive, the emergence of a working class movement, and the political involvement of an upper and middle class intelligentsia inspired by visions of a socialist society.[6]

Since the early theatrical works pioneered by Bastian and De Silva which became very popular during the first three decades of the twentieth century, a melodramatic theatre emerged, characterized by "copious sob-stuff, multiple murders and suicides, glamorized sexual promiscuities and drinking and gambling scenes", interspersed with "aphrodisiac jokes".[7] The first Sinhala films which appeared during the late 1940s also carried the same tradition with the added

---

[5] K N O Dharmadasa, *"The Peradeniya Contribution to Literature, Theatre and the Arts"* in K M de Silva and G H Peiris eds. *The University System in Sri Lanka: Vision and Reality*, Kandy, International Centre for Ethnic Studies, 1995, pp 130-44.

[6] K N O Dharmadasa, *"Literature and the Arts"* in K M de Silva ed. Silva ed. *"Sri Lanka: A Survey*, C. Hust & Co., London, 1977, pp 434-46.

[7] Wilmot P Wijetunga "The Future of Sinhalese Drama" in Ananda Tissa de Alwis (ed.) *"Souvenir of the festival of Arts*, 1949, pp 12-16.

disadvantage of being heavily influenced by South Indian cinema with its own formula of melodrama, love scenes, fights, songs dances and low comedy.[8]

Similarly the poetry in the late 19th and early 20th centuries were characterised by a pre-occupation with patriotic and revivalist themes and a verse form which it had yet to free itself of classical prosody and diction. During the 1940s there emerged, as in the novel and the theatre, a populist movement of poetry which came to be known as the Colombo school who often tried to depict "an impossible dream-world where one finds only moonlight, cool water, flowers, music and love"[9]

Nevertheless from about the early 1940s some poets of the Colombo school and some fiction writers, including W A Silva himself, showed a growing concern for the poor and the down-trodden in society. This concern is partly explained by the influence of the Marxist political movement in the island which began in mid 1930s with the establishment of *Lanka Sama Samaja* Party (LSSP), the first modern Marxist party in the island. At the same time there appears to have been the direct influence of western literature, since English literacy was spreading with the rapid expansion of secondary education during the 1930s and 40s.[10]

This sympathetic concern with the poorer sections of society is seen in some poems of P B Alwis Perera (1917-1966). The following translations are from his collection of poems *Vedanava* (Pain, 1946).

A handful own estates and paddy lands,
Nine tenths do not own even a square foot.
Some born on this land of Lanka know only Kurakkan[11]
And have never seen rice.
A man with a son who has no brains
Spends his wealth to give him an education
A poor man's intelligent son
Can be no more than a labourer.

---

[8] The Report of the Commission of Inquiry into the Film Industry, *Sessional Papers* II (1965), Colombo Govt. Press. p. 68.

[9] S A S Gunasinghe "*The New Note in Contemporary Sinhalese Poetry*" in *The Observer Annual,* 1950, pp 70-75.

[10] See C R de Silva, *"Sri Lankan: A History"*, New Delhi, Vikas, 1987, pp 212-13.

[11] Kurakkan is Indian millet, a rough cereal which has a slightly bitter taste.

Outside the gate beyond the mansion's compound
A beggar woman lies stretched with her child
People of the mansion sitting amidst meats and milk
Are feeding half a dozen dogs, their pets.

In this collection there are separate pieces dealing with the common worker — character types such as the employee of a small shop, the rickshawman and the blacksmith; also there are pieces entitled "labourer's family", on the poor man's diet which included gram worth "one cent", "confessions of a prostitute", "the tears of the farmer", and "child suffering form hunger". Poems with similar concern with the lot of the poorer sections of society appeared in the poetry journals, *Miivadaya, Dedunna and Suvanda* which were very popular during the 1940s and 50s. Some of the novels and short stories of the period excoriate the privileged sections of society, the professionals, the businessmen and the richer folk in villages, for their exploitation of the poor. A similar trend was seen in some of the theatrical productions of the early 1940s. Such castigations of the upper strata of society were also seen in contemporary Sri Lankan Tamil literature.[12]

The principal trend in the Sinhala novel during the late 1950s and early 1960s was the depiction of psychological traumas arising out of the conflict between the old and the new during a period of rapid social transformation. In Martin Wickramasinghe's *Viragaya* (1956) we find depicted the spiritual dilemmas of a sensitive Sinhalese youth, brought up in a traditional household, confronted with the responsibilities of adulthood in a rapidly modernizing society. Subsequently several novels were to appear with "anti heroes" as the dominant characters. These include: Ediriweera Sarathchandra's *Malagiya Atto* (1957), and *Valmat Vi Hasarak Nudutim* (1963), Gunadasa Amarasekera's *Yali Upannemi* (1960), *Depa Noladdo* (1961) and *Gandabba Apadanaya* (1964), Siri Gunasinghe's *Hevanalla* (1960), Madavala Ratnayake's *Sita Nati Bambalova* (1961) and K Jayatilaka's *Parajitayo* (1960) and *Aparasanna Kathavak* (1962).

Soon a strong reaction against this trend was to emerge in some quarters. There were two major reasons for this development:

---

[12] See K N O Dharmadasa, *"Literature and the Arts"* p. 438.

one was a charge against certain prominent literary men, notabl those connected with University of Peradeniya that they were pa of a literary cabal promoting "decadent" foreign literary ideologie to the detriment of the national tradition.[13] Secondly, couple with this was an ideological movement which sought to promot a "socialist" literary ideology. Martin Wickramasinghe who visite the Soviet Union in the late 1950s on an invitation from the literar establishment in that country published a book entitled *Sovie Deshaye Naegima* ("The Rise of the Soviet Union", Maharagma Saman Press) in 1963. Among other things it was a long descriptio of the "socialist realist" literary ideology which had been eagerl promoted during the Stalinist era and for quite some time after hi death.[14] Several other writers followed the lead given b Wickramasinghe. The introspective writings of Sarathchandr and others were castigated as "capitalist" and "decadent" as the were not concerned with the burgeoning problems faced b the common man. It was urged that this "ivory tower" attitud be replaced by an "art for the people" which would encourag them in their "struggle against imperialism, neo-colonialism an capitalism".[15]

By the 1960s we notice the social concerns of Sinhala writer becoming more and more pronounced. This could have been due t the influence of the concept of socialist realism, or, perhaps it coul have been also a natural development of realistic portrayal of socia movements, which began with Wickramasinghe's *Gamperaliya* (1944). For example, in Sarathchandra's novel *Valmat Vi Hasara Nudutim* (1963) the author deals with rootlessness in the Englis educated class in Sri Lankan society. The novelist Jayatilaka in hi *Parajitiyo* (1960) and *Delovata Nati Aya* (1964) deals with aspect of the work of leftist political parties, and appears to question th genuineness of some Marxist ideologues who pose as saviours of th poor and the down-trodden.

---

13 *Ibid*, pp 442-3.

14 See *Soviet Deshaye Naegima*, pp 184-220.

15 See for example, Karunasena Jayalath, *Sahityaya Kalava Ha Janathava*, Colomb 1967 and Gunasena Vitana, "Samajavadi Yatharthaya Ha Sinhala Navakathava" i Palita Gunasinghe (ed.) *Sri Lanka Visva Vidyala Sangarava*, Colombo, 1969, pp. 24-26.

With Sarathchandra's *Heta Eccara Kaluvara Nae* (1971) and Jayatilaka's *Matu Sambandhayi* (1975) we find direct discussions about the factors that led to the youth insurrection in 1971 in which several thousand people died. Although the insurrection itself is not treated in detail we notice glimpses of the poverty and hopelessness of the educated youth who became fascinated by a revolutionary ideology which advocated the overthrow, by violent means, of a state system which they believed could not bring them equality and social justice.

In the *Gandabba Apadanaya* (1964) by Gunadasa Amarasekera we find for the first time an attempt to portray Sinhala Tamil relations which had become an acute political problem from the 1950s. The hero, a Sinhalese administrative officer, falls in love with a Tamil doctor and the trials and tribulations of this love affair is portrayed with great sympathy and understanding.

Sugathapala De Silva's *Ballo bat Kati* (1976) and H A Seneviratne's *Elivenava Nodene* (1978) deal with the intrigues and hypocritical attitudes of political leaders who pose as champions of the poor and underprivileged in society. *Elivenava Nodene* is of particular interest because of its sympathetic portrayal of the social and economic problems faced by the peasantry. The author focuses attention on many of the common problems faced by the peasantry in the Kandyan areas of Sri Lanka, such as landlessness, lack of education, un-employment or under-employment and drunkenness. It is interesting to note how he depicts the relationship between the Tamil labourers and the Sinhala peasantry. The author strives to show the fact that both groups have similar economic and social problems and that their circumstances often prompt them to work together to solve them.

Gunasene Vitana, who has done a great deal to popularize the concept of socialist realism among the Sinhala reading public, published a novel entitled *Pamaa Novii Vaehaepan Vaehi Valaavee* in 1975 in which he tried to trace political developments in Sri Lanka during the period 1940-65. Set in a village, with tea estates in the Southern Province, the novel depicted the class struggle between the estate owners and the labourers. With characters from the upper class who throw in their lot with the poor, on the one hand and with those from among the poor who collaborate with the land-owners on the other, the author seems to suggest the following message articulated by a person form the upper class who organizes a strike and who is approached by a relative reminding him of their kinship ties:

> "The only relationship a man could have is the relationship based on class. You happened to be brother of mine, a long time ago. But now I consider only the poor who cannot even have one meal a day, as my relatives ..." (p.35)

Vitana's *Viplavaye Kaerali Kaarayoo* (1979) is a very explicit examination of the causes that led to the 1971 insurgency. It documents the failure of the elected governments, right-wing and left-wing, to provide a fair deal to the educated youth as well as a litany of their serious shortcomings; bribery, corruption and misappropriation of public funds. He argues that all this paves the way for the mobilization of a sizeable section of the youth by the radical JVP movement. Similarly Sunanada Mahendra in his *Idoraya* (1978) reveals the corruption, favouritism, harassment of the innocent and political revenge that goes on in contemporary Sri Lankan society.[16]

The Position of Women

In the traditional cultures of South Asia women were generally treated as objects of beauty, while at the same time it was believed that their position in society was to be determined by men. The well known statement of Manu, that during childhood a woman is under the protection of the father, and in her youth under that of the husband and in her old age under that of the son epitomizes this traditional attitude. In addition, religions which upheld celibacy as an ideal saw women as an obstacle in the path of higher spiritual attainments. Thus we find many stories in classical Sinhalese literature portraying this negative attitude to women. Here we must state that the traditional Buddhist attitude was not all that rigid. The Buddha had encouraged the founding of a order of nuns and

---

16 See U P Meddegama, "The Political Novel in Sinhalese" in *Sri Lanka Journal of the Humanities*, XVI, 1 and 2, 1990, pp. 67-86.

some of them had achieved the highest spiritual status, that of Arahantshi.[17] Even in classical Sinhalese literature we find positive portrayals of women characters: for example that of Visakha, one of the chief lay devotees of the Buddha.

In the Sinhalese novel that emerged during late 19th century we find some of the positive aspects of women's character being portrayed in spite of the fact that the authors upheld a traditionalist viewpoint. For example in *Meena* by A Simon De Silva, *Vimala* (1892) by Albert De Silva and *Jayatissa Saha Roslin* (1905) of Piyadasa Sirisena, we find women acting with a great deal of self confidence and independence. Thus it is obvious that the social transformation which was taking place at the time prompted the novelists to adopt a more balanced view of the role of women in society.

As the Sinhalese novel developed in the 20th century with sophistication in technique, and an expansion of the themes dealt with in them, we find women characters being portrayed with deeper understanding. For example, Nanda in Wickramasinghe's *Gamperaliya* (1944) Sarojini and Bati in his own *Viragaya* (1956) and Soma in Gunadasa Amarasekera's *Karumakkarayo* (1955) are striking examples of vividly portrayed women.

Women novelists began appearing in the Sinhala literary scene from the 1960s and thereafter we find greater emphasis being placed in the problems faced by women in society. Among these novelists special mention should be made of Sumitra Rahubaddha, Aileen Siriwardene, Eva Ranaweera, Sita Wijesuriya and Anula Wijeratne Menike. The greater interest in women's problems would have been augmented by contemporary world trends. Sumitra Rahubaddha, probably the foremost women novelist in Sri Lanka today has been quite explicit in what she sought to achieve in her novels. For example:

1. "My principal concern in the novel *Bumuturunu* ("Carpets", 1978) was to focus the attention of the reader on the character of Lilavati. When her family faces disintegration due to the lethargy of Chandrasena it is her determination that helps to prevent this and preserve its integrity."

---

[17] K M I Swarnasinghe, *Sri Lankuvu Vargika Aragalaya Pilibimbu Kala Padya Ha Gita Nirmana*, Colombo, Godage Brothers, 1992, pp. 28-29.

2. "Through *Udanaya* ("Paen", 1979) I sought to uphold the self-respect, strength of character, and courage of Amaralatha who stood unshaken in the face of sorrow, tears and heart-break. Confronted with harrowing economic and social problems she did not act as one who had lost her moorings."
3. "In my *Dala Rala Pela* ('Strong Line of Waves', 1981) I tried to portray the self confidence, self respect and virtues of womanhood as represented by Pabavati which stood stead-fastly in the face of the conspicuous wickedness of men-folk."

These statements do not mean that the characters Rahubuddha has portrayed are mere puppets. In the final analyses it is the social forces against which both men and women struggle against that determine the fate of the characters. In *Dala Rala Pela* for example, a nineteen year old girl is forced to become the mistress of an old man due to her poverty. Later she falls in love with a young man but he becomes a victim of economic difficulties. It is against there odds that she had to struggle while safeguarding her self-respect. Similarly in *Udanaya*, Amaralatha, the heroine, through no fault of hers is deserted by her husband. She overcomes a strong inner urge to plead with him not to desert her and their child, realising that this would be of no use and that she would be merely demeaning herself in that attempt.

Among the male novelists who have attempted to make special attempts to deal with some of the problems faced by present day Sri Lankan society, the most notable are Somaweera Senanayake and Aravvala Nandimitra. For example in Senanayake's *Mavakage Gitaya* ("The Song of a Mother", 1975) the conflict between a traditionalist mother in law and a daughter-in-law who tries to assert her independence is portrayed with deep understanding. In Senanayake's plot the reader is given the impression that the attitude of the older woman is the result of a lack of education and her limited experiences about society. Unlike what would have happened in older times, the son, prompted by his wife, leaves the mother and sets up his own household. Here the predicament of the mother evokes our sympathy, and we are left with the conclusion that the root of the problem is social backwardness.

Nandimitra's *Maldeniye Simion* (1975) and *Padmavati* (1979) depict the sad predicament of women faced with poverty and destitution. Somawathi in *Maldeniye Simion* is forced to become a prostitute in order to support her aged father and younger sister. Padmavati in the other novel has no alternative but to marry a man who befriends her when her husband dies suddenly. The man turns out to be a monster who not only ill treats her but also rapes his step-daughter.

Sumitra Rahubaddha's *Iti Pahan* ("Candles", 1994) which depicts the life story of a girl revolutionary of the 1987 insurgency. The illegitimate daughter of a white man, and his servant woman the heroine who is endowed with beauty as well as intelligence grows up as a social misfit and is drawn into the movement due to the kindness and understanding she gets from some group members. Her love affair with a young man of a traditional household ends in failure and she finally marries a former class-mate who is intellectually very much inferior to her. Family conflicts ensue as he fails to understand her involvement with the revolutionary movement and in a fit of rage he commits suicide. As the insurgency is in progress the forces of state become active opposing it and she too becomes one of their victims. The character of the heroine of *Iti Pahan* appears to be symbolic of the ideological forces that led to the insurgency. As the portrayal of an unusual and admirable character however, the novel assumes the dimensions of a tragic drama.

In recent years Sinhala cinema too has reflected the current concern about the predicament of women in modern society. Two films stand out in this regard *Maarutaya* ("Wind", 1995) and *Ayoma* (1995). *Maarutaya* recounts the fate of three upper-class women who become victims of social change when their family disintegrates after the death of the male who was its mainstay. He, a leading politician, is defeated at an election and dies soon after. The middle aged wife, has to lead a secret life of prostitution in order to keep up her former life-style,. A similar fate awaits one of the daughters who eventually becomes the mistress of a brothel-keeper. The other daughter escapes such a fate because she has a chance to go abroad where she marries and leads a respectable life. The two daughters come together finally for the mother's funeral and they recount the story of their family. In the course of the story we get glimpses of unsavoury aspects of the current political culture, such as, bribery and corruption, harassment and even assassination of political opponents. In *Ayoma* (1995) the focus is on a poor village girl whose tragic life of being sexually exploited as it unfolds gives glimpses of the corruption, selfishness and inhumanity in all walks of life. Starting with her being raped by a politician who promises her employment she falls prey to many others, particularly "respectable" men, including a Buddhist monk. A child born to her is sold to a foreign couple. The only man who genuinely loves her dies in an accident. The struggle of the woman Ayoma to rise up and continue after each fall is depicted with great understanding and when her tragic end is reached the audience is left with a powerful feeling of the stark reality of the enormous difficulties of women struggling for self-respect in a male dominated society.

The Theatre

Sinhala theatre has been by far the most vigorous of artistic activities in recent years and it has been very much the politicized of all the arts. While the "art theatre" created by modernizing pioneers such as Ediriweera Sarachchandra and Dayananda Gunawardana, still draws large audiences, it is the theatre with a socio-political focus, the creation of a younger generation of writer-directors such as Sugathapala de Silva, Henry Jayasena, Ranjit Dharmakeerthi, Jayalath Manoratne, Simon Nawagattegama, Jayantha Chandrasiri and K B Herath that has become the most vibrant factor in the modern theatrical tradition and also most popular with the present day audience. While it is to the credit of Sarachchandra, Gunawardana and a few others connected with the University of Peradeniya that they raised the Sinhala theatre to a sophisticated art form, with well constructed scripts on serious themes, tasteful productions and talented acting during the 1950s and the sixties, the popularity of the genre and the high level of rapport with the audiences led to a more politically conscious theatre dealing with themes of contemporary significance.

Sarachchandra, widely acknowledged as the father of modern Sinhala theatre, usually selected his themes from myth, legend and history and concentrated on perennial human problems such as relationships between men and women and conflict of generations. But some others who followed him, notably Henry Jayasena and Sugathapala De Silva turned to socially relevant current themes. Two early examples are Jayasena's *Janelaya* ("The Window", 1961) and *Boding Kaarayoo* ("The Boarders", 1962). Both of them focused attention on the life of the urban middle-class with their daily frustrations due to low pay, the snobbery of superior officers and the cut-throat competition among peers. Once these two plays were well received by the audiences, Jayasena and De Silva staged several more plays with themes dealing with similar contemporary problems. Jayasena's *Mana Ranjana Waeda Warjana* ("Delightful Strikes", 1966) and *Apata Pute Magak Naetee* ("Son, We Have No Future", 1968) and De Silva's *Nil Katrol Mal* ("The Blue Katrol Flowers") and *Dunna Dunugamuve* ("Weapons are Not in Hand", 1972) are worth mentioning. *Mana Ranjana Waeda Warjana and Dunna Dunugamuve* dealt with problems faced by the working class in strike situations. *Nil Katrol Mal* was about the family life of middle class men working in urban offices and *Apata Pute* was based on a true story where a university student committed suicide due to financial difficulties.

The 1970s saw the proliferation of plays with a propagandist intent. This could be explained by the political background where the United Left Front with an avowed Marxist programme of economic development was in power and there was a conscious attempt by the government to promote a socialist ideology through mass media. As could be expected, most of the theatre productions containing political "messages" were of poor quality. The most outstanding theatrical productions of the early 1970s was *Suba Saha Yasa* ("Suba and Yasa", 1974) by Simon Nawagattegama, portraying a human drama in the aftermath of a "revolution" where the leader once in power becomes the prisoner of a well established system of tradition, protocol and bureaucracy. Although a tremendous success artistically as well as in box office ratings, it was condemned by the "socialist" critics as a decadent work which undermined the revolutionary commitment that was the need of the day.

The change of government in 1977 which brought to power the more liberal and rightist UNP saw dramatists again concentrating on social and cultural problems. Somalatha Subasinghe in her *Vikurti* ("Distortions", 1982) drew attention to the rat race in today's educational system where children are mercilessly goaded for higher achievements by over-ambitious parents. In *Tala Mala Pipila* ("The Talipot Palm Blooms", 1985) Jayalath Manoratne warned about the disintegration of traditional human values in the face of rapid commercialization which was taking place due to the "open" economic policy of the government. The Talipot palm blooms once every thirty or forty years. The moment of efflorescence — the flower is almost opulently beautiful — is also moment of death, for the tree dies thereafter.

In the mid-eighties there were two tendencies at work in Sinhala theatre. One was a growing concern about a threat to democracy due to certain acts of a government which commanded four-fifths of the seats in parliament, and which had adopted a new constitution with an Executive Presidency. Several plays depicting monsters against whom everybody is helpless were produced, such as, *Mooraa* ("The Shark") by Jayantha Chandrasiri, *Eekaa Adhipathy* ("The Dictator") by Dharmasiri Bandaranayake and *Makaraakshaya* ("The Dragon Demon") also by Dharmasiri Bandaranayake. The other trend was the emergence of a commercial pot-boiler, as if the audiences were keen to go in for some kind of escapism. The first and the most popular of these plays was Sergeant Nallathamby, satirizing a Tamil police sergeant with many hilarious situations and a dialogue full of double meaning. *Neyinage Suuduwa* ("The Gambligh Den of Neyina") and *Raaja Kapuru* were two others of the same type.

In 1988 there was another political change — there was an island-wide terror campaign unleashed by the Janatha Vimukthi Peramuna a group of Sinhala Marxists cum nationalists and, at the height of their campaigns characterized by political assassinations, work stoppages and closure of schools, a presidential election was held and a new Executive President was elected. The new president, R Premadasa was well known as a hard task-master and the government in a bid to crush the terrorist movement adopted a severely repressive policy meeting terror with terror. There was a widespread feeling that any form of dissent led to severe reprisals. Hence dramatists sought to give expression to their concern for the future of democracy by resorting to ingenious means.

Sudu Saha Kalu ("Black and White") written by Simon Nawagattegama and produced by Sriyanth Mendis narrated a story in South Africa. In depicting the repression of blacks by whites; gruelling torture scenes, and abductions and extra-judicial killings, were put on stage. It was obvious that the playwright's intent was to bring about a cathartic effect since such atrocities had become well known in the contemporary situation. Other plays with similar characteristics were *Panchayuda* ("Five Weapons", 1990) by Linton Semage; *Platoon* by Ranjith De Silva, (1990), *Naga Gurula* ("Killer of Snakes", 1991) by K B Herath; *Yadam* ("Chains", 1992 a translation of an African play) produced by Somalatha Subasinghe; *Dhavala Bhiishanam* ("White Terror", 1992, a translation of Men without Shadows by Satre) produced by Dharmasiri Bandaranayake; *Ottukaarayo* ("The Spy", 1993) by Jayantha Chandrasiri; *Yakshagamanaya* ("The Arrival of the Demons", 1994) by Sunil Wijesirirwardene and Dharmasiri Bandaranayake and *Adhipathiyage Marana Manchakaya* ("The Death Bed of The Boss", 1994) by Buddhika Damayanthi.

To get an impression of the kind of theme with its innuendoes I give below a description of *Naga Gurula* which has been very popular since it was first staged in 1991. The story is enacted in the form of a play within a play. There was a troupe of actors which disintegrated because all had run away fearing for their lives. A lone actor comes on stage and starts narrating the story of a play they used to enact. It was set in South America during the time of the Spanish conquests. The Spanish had established their hegemony over an unsuspecting and innocent population and commercial exploitation ensues. A winery had been established and the natives are forced to give up their traditional agriculture for work in the winery. Protests by them are ruthlessly crushed by armed thugs. People go "missing" and it transpires that they are drowned in the huge vats of the winery. The owner of the winery, a ruthless tyrant, pretends publicly to be humane while carrying on his campaign of terror. There is a particular scene where he comes to offer his pious condolences to the widow of a native chieftain who obviously had been murdered by this own minors. In the context of the socio-political atmosphere of the early nineties, the innuendo was obvious. Thus the Sinhala theatre had become largely a "protest theatre".

Sinhala theatre whose major concern has been political, i.e., exposing and satirizing undemocratic trends in the political system, picked a feminist theme in 1995 with K B Herath's *Dona Catherina.* It was based on the life of Dona Catherina (1578-1613) the only surviving heir/heiress, to the throne of Kandy at the time. The Portuguese, under whose protection she grew up, first tried to get her married to a protege of theirs. Next she fell into the hands of an ambitious chieftain Vimaladharmasuriya who killed the Portuguese protege and make himself the king of Kandy. Dona Catherina bore him a son and two daughters. At his untimely death in 1604 his foster brother, a Buddhist monk, disrobed and married her so that his claim to the throne could be made secure. She had three children by him.

Subsequently, her eldest son, by the former king secretly murdered her second husband so that his own sons would be the heirs to the throne. Heart-broken Dona Catherina falls ill and before she dies she hears the news that her own daughter is being married to the king so that his claim to the throne is kept secure. The tragic life of Dona Catherina highlights the plight of woman in the traditional male dominated society. She and her daughter are mere tools in the game of power-politics. The playwright has dramatized this predicament of women to show that in the political game there is no place for the likes, dislikes, and feelings of women.

Sinhala Tamil Relations — Ethic Tensions and Conflicts

While it is possible to notice a souring of relations between the Sinhalese and the Tamils from about the mid 1950s real conflict situation emerged only in the 1980s. The possibility of a conflict was becoming obvious after about 1972, when separatist movements emerged in the Tamil community. In such a context we find several artists focusing attention on the need to foster inter-communal harmony. The most striking example of this concern was the film *Sarungale* ("The Kite", 1978) by a young director Sunil Ariyaratne. It centres round the life of Nadarajah, a middle aged government employee, who like thousands of other Sri Lankan Tamils, lives in Colombo, amidst the Sri Lankan populace. Nadarajah is a large hearted man who had decided to remain a bachelor since his love-affair with a Sinhala woman failed because it was opposed by the families of both. He himself faced the fact that his sister, who lives in their ancestral home in Jaffna, married a low-caste man. Confronted with family opposition she eventually commits suicide. Nadarajah is well known, in the Sinhalese neighbourhood of a Colombo suburb where he lives alone, as a friendly man who helps everybody with their problems. One if his very good friends is Simon, a local thug who had been helped by Nadarajah on many an occasion. An ethnic riot occurs and the people in the neighbourhood come to his rescue. Looters from another vicinity try to enter Nadarajah's house and they are prevented from doing so by Simon. Nadarajah advised by his neighbours not to venture out does not heed their advice, since he strongly believes that as he had been good with the Sinhalese people nobody will harm him. One day while returning from work, he is attacked on the way, is severely injured and breathes his last in the hands of Simon. *Sarunagale* dramatizes a well known situation in many Sinhalese areas during the ethnic riots of the fifties, sixties, and seventies where Sinhala people came to the rescue of Tamils who had been living amidst them for decades. The theme has been handled with great finesse and the role of Nadarajah had been portrayed very effectively by the veteran actor Gamini Fonseka.

Other artists of the period, particularly poets, took up the theme of the need for inter-communal harmony. Parakrama Kodituwakku, an established Sinhalese poet published a collection of Sinhala and Tamil poetry entitled *Indu-Lanka* in 1979. A veteran Sinhala writer K G Amaradasa is well known for his attempts to introduce Tamil poets to the Sinhala reading public. His translations of Tamil poetry appeared often in the poetry page of the Sinhala weekly *Divayina*. Similarly, Dominic Jeeva, a Tamil poet living in Jaffna, a published translations of Sinhala poetry in the journal *Mallihei* which he edited during the 1980s. The Janatha Lekhaka Peramuna, a Marxist literary organization, look up the theme of inter-communal harmony, in such works as *Demala Keti Katha Ekatuva* (1979)—a collection of translations form Tamil short stories: Particular mention should be made of Gunasena Witana, the secretary of JLP who as early as 1971 published "*Palama*" ("The Bridge") a story emphasizing the need for inter-communal harmony, in a collection of short stories entitled *Aiya Wage Kenek*. His own collection of short stories *Sinhala piyakuta Dava Demala Mavakage Kusa Upan Puthkuge Kath Vastuva* ("the story of a son born to a Tamil mother by a Sinhala father") appeared in 1984. There are two stories in this collection which depict the poignant side of the ethnic divide. One of them, which gives the whole collection its name, recounts the story of a young man and his sister caught in the conflict between the two communities. Their parents, a Sinhalese father and the Tamil mother, had fallen in love at the time they were studying in the university and had married and begotten children not knowing the fate that would befall the whole family in the future. The family was living in Jaffna when the ethnic conflict erupted and immediately they become the target of extremist elements. They decide to come and live in the South, amidst the Sinhala community where they are harassed too. The father's health fails due to the harassment the family under-goes and he dies a disappointed man and the heart broken mother follows him. The sister marries a Tamil. When the next wave of ethnic violence comes about the brother loses track of the sister and her husband and he comes to know subsequently that they are no longer among the living. The tragic story of the family unfolds in diary notes kept by the brother who is finally an inmate in a psychiatric hospital. The other story is about a Tamil barber in a Southern village. There was a time, before the ethnic conflicts came about from the fifties onwards, when practically all the barbers in the island were Tamils, and wherever they set up their barber-shops they became fully integrated into the local society, many of them marrying Sinhalese wives. This story is about those times at which the author looks back in nostalgia.

Of all the arts, it is in the field of poetry that we find the most frequent references to the need for inter-ethnic harmony. Some of these poems have been set to music. One of them whose first-lines are

Uturu kone numba hinaehen Nadarajah Malliye
Dakunu kone numba hinaehen Sumanasiri malliye
("at the north end you smile brother Nadarajah
At the south end you smile brother Sumanasiri")

is very popular even today and is often broadcast over the radio.

Interestingly, the aftermath of the in ethnic riots of July 1983, there has been a spate of poems published in the weekly Sinhala newspapers *Divayina* and *Silumina* on the sense of ethnic harmony. Also, it has been observed that in other newspapers, daily as well as weekly, there have been occasional poems which depicted the nation's shock about this inhuman behaviour of a small group of extremists. The following is a translation of one such poem by well known Sinhalese poet Dharmasiri Rajapakse.[18]

The Tear which I left at the Times

When I was passing the line [rooms][19] one evening
I heard the cry of an infant
Since there was a fence to our relationship
A pain arose inside and I left a tear as I departed.

The full moon of the Asela month [20]
Terrified at so much bloodshed
Having seen blazing swords and cudgels
And the dastardly scuffle and sacrifice
Tamil mothers clasping to their breasts
Children who were like their own life.

Running away to escape
From blood-thirsty men chasing behind

Another evening I stood near the burned down line [rooms]
And thought about a tomorrow without fires

---

18 Ranjini Obeyesekere, "The Sinhala Theatre of the Eighties: A Forum for Criticism", The Sri Lanka Journal of the Humanities, Vols. xvii and xviii, Golden Jubilee Commemoration Double Volume, 1994, pp. 75-89; Michael Fernando, "Politicization of the Sinhala Theatre and Class in post-independent Sri Lanka," Samar, No. 4, Winter, 1994, pp. 16-19.

19 "Lines" (Sinhala "Laeyima") is the name given to a row of small houses which housed Tamil workers and their families in the tea and rubber plantations.

20 "Asela" according to the Sinhala calendar in July and August.

Although the infant that cried that day
Did not cry, I cried myself that evening.

Similarly, there were poetic responses to incidents such as the massacre of Sinhalese at the Dollar and Kent farms in October 1984, the massacre of Sinhalese at the Sri Maha Bodhi Temple in Anuradhapura, car bombs exploding in Colombo in 1985 and the 1986 killing of over a hundred people in one instance, and over thirty in another and the massacre of 48 Buddhist monks at Arantalawa in 1987 all perpetrated by terrorist groups associated with the LTTE, in the regular poetry page of the weekly *Divayina* and *Silumina*. It was observed that poets tried to look at these incidents from different angles. Some condemned them, some were expressing a sense of shock and horror and others pondered on the inability of men to live together in peace and harmony.[21]

When the Indo-Lanka Peace Accord was signed by Prime Minister Rajiv Gandhi of India and President J R Jayewardene of Sri Lanka there was a mixed reaction. It was condemned by some activists, particularly the Sinhalese extremist organization the Janatha Vimukthi Peramuna (JVP) while others saw in it a glimmer of hope for a peaceful tomorrow. The following is the translation of a poem by a Buddhist monk, pallegama Hemaratna, who incidentally was an inmate of the Sri Maha Bodhi Temple of Anuradhapura where two years previously LTTE gunmen had massacred 146 people including some bhikshus:

Having dispelled the darkness
In both army camps
The moon beams of peace
Are kissing tree tops

In this gentle night
Enemy minds are appeased
At the hour of day-break
The morning is beautiful

Minds wet with
Compassion and Love
Fires of hatred are extinguished
Nestling humane feelings

---

[21] Swarnasinghe, *op. cit.* p. 29.

Doors and windows thrown open
Morning light peeps inside
Doves nestle near at hand

Rugged paths have ended
Gentle white flowers bloom
Gardens are smiling
Full of pollen and fragrance
This is no dream dear friends
This is reality.

THE CONTEMPORARY ART SCENE IN SRI LANKA

Stanley Kirinde

Introduction

The contemporary art scene in Sri Lanka embraces many areas of artistic activity such as music; dancing; drama; cinema; graphic art; industrial design and commercial art; ceramic work and other crafts; and painting and sculpture. These subjects are provided as courses of study at the University of Kelaniya and at the Institute of Aesthetic Studies of that University. As these subjects cannot be covered in a brief article, it is proposed to confine this essay to the subject of contemporary painting only.

A brief survey of the recent past of the field of painting in Sri Lanka should help in appreciating the contemporary scene. To begin with we could consider the developments in the period before the island became independent in 1948 after a century and half of British rule.

The significant developments in the pre-1947 era can be considered under three broad categories. First, we observe the almost total demise by the end of the 19th Century, of the native tradition of painting. This tradition was a very ancient one, which, over a period of more than two thousand years, developed as a refined style of mural painting applied largely to the presentation of Buddhist subject matter in an easily understood form on the walls of temples and caves. Perhaps a notable exceptional to this traditional and religious painting are the 5th Century paintings of about 20 female figures in a niche on the Sigiriya rock in a central Sri Lanka. This ancient tradition of mural painting can divided into two phases. Firstly, there are the classical works found mainly at Sigiriya, done in the 5th century and those at Polonnaruwa done in the 12th Century. Secondly, there are the medieval paintings done in the period between the 14th-19th Centuries. Broadly speaking the medieval work while being very decorative, sparkling and vigorous are less graceful and sophisticated than the paintings of earlier period. These paintings, both classical and medieval are much like the work at Ajantha and the temple murals of South India.

The native Sri Lankan tradition faded painting faded away quickly during the 19th century under the impact of the current popular styles of painting which were introduced into the island by its British rulers after the rebellion of 1848. It was the newness of the western style of painting which is referred to rather loosely as "Academic Art", which made it possible for the new style to undermine and supplant the Sri Lankan tradition. And, this new style was able to win over not only the westernised native community living in the cities, principally in the capital of Colombo, but also many country folk and even the class of mural artists known as *Sitharas* who for generations had practised the ancient art of temple painting.

The Nineteenth Century Impact of Western Styles

The compelling nature of the impact of the new European style of painting during the colonial era is conveyed in the observations made by a German visitor to the island — Earnest Haeckles. In his book "*A Visit to Ceylon in 1882*" he says that "dealing" with the natives

> for natural objects was most interesting ... when we agreed to barter. I had with me a number of small articles for the purpose. But the highest value was attributed to coloured prints ... and this says much for the artistic feeling of the Çingalese. They were immensely admired ... highly prized as return for presents and hospitality. Before long I found the best huts in the village (Weligama in South Sri Lanka) decorated with the products of German art ... headman came to call ... in the hope of receiving the much coveted prints.

> First in estimation stood the military — Prussian, Austrian, French, English and so forth. Next came theatrical figure; fancy portraits; then came pictures of animals; and last of all landscapes etc., the gaudier the better"

Thus with the dissemination of such examples of popular western art, it is not difficult to understand the ease with which the native style of painting lost its appeal. But when the temple paintings done in the western or academic manner in the late 19th and early 20th centuries are examined it will be evident that their activity more often than not have failed to assimilate the new imported style.

For, these paintings do not 'indicate the Western dynamic mastery of the subject; nor the understanding of Western colour harmony; nor the scientific laws of perspective and anatomy. Only, a rather naive charm animates the new paintings, but this is of little recompense for the destruction of the virile native-tradition.

The second category under which the pre-1947 painting can be surveyed is the Revivalist movement of the 1930's. The larger objective of this movement was the rehabilitation of Buddhism. In painting it led to a striking achievement, the painting of a series of murals on the walls of the Buddhist vihara of Kelaniya (in the outskirts of Colombo) in a manner which attempted to revive the classical Sinhala tradition of moral pointing found at Sigiriya and Pollonnaruwa, and perhaps the Ajantha tradition as well, which the painter Solias Mendis is said to have studied on a visit to India prior to undertaking the painting of the Kelaniya temple. There paintings are today enormously popular and are undoubtedly impressive in scale and number. But a proper aesthetic evaluation of the work has yet to be done.

The "43-Group" and Its Impact

The third category which has how to be considered is by far the most important in view of its immediate significance for the understanding of the contemporary Sri Lankan art scene. In the 1930's a group of radical artists — Harry Peiris, Justin Deraniyagala, George Keyt; Ivan Peiris; Richard Gabriel; Beling; Collette; Classen and Manjusiri with the patronage and assistance of Lionel Wendt an artist of the camera, embarked on a mission to educate the art-loving public and popularize the developments in European art in this century — i.e., the art we call 'Modern Art'. With this objective in view they formed in 1943 the art society named the '43 Group". The formation of this group is perhaps the most important event in the field of art in this century. After 1943 the public and artists of Sri Lanka came to be increasingly familiar with the movements of modern art such as: Cubism; Surrealism; Futurism; Abstract Expressionism and other new movements and theories of art. The painters of the "43 Group" were all outstanding artists. A measure of their importance as artists is evident in the reaction to their work of John Berger of the New Statesman, when he reviewed their exhibition in England in 1952. Berger went to the extent of saying that "In terms of their art they are trying to do nothing less than to solve the problem of a world revolution. That they occasionally succeed is far more significant than that they sometimes fail. My interest comes from my belief that Asia, rather than Europe will be the first to resolve a new, truly democratic tradition in Art." And, at about the same time William Graham commented in the Art-magazine *Studio*, that "the most significant movement in Eastern Art today is to be found in Ceylon". The "43 Group" artists were certainly not overwhelmed by the European movements. They were innovators being acutely conscious of the island's rich cultural heritage, and each member of the group was able to evolve his own modern yet personal style with a distinct local flavour.

The most striking example in the island today of the application of a modern style in painting are the wall paintings executed by the most celebrated member of the "43 Group" George Keyt at the Gotami Vihara in Borella, a suburb of Colombo. Keyt's temple paintings like those done by Solias Mendis at Kelaniya were inspired by the Buddhist revivalist movement of the time. But while at Kelaniya the attempt was to restore an old tradition, at the Gotami Vihara there was a serious attempt to create a new tradition by presenting an Eastern subject, the life of the Buddha, in a Cubistic manner.

It is of some interest to note that during the years when in the world of Sri Lankan painting there was a revivalist movement as well as a modern movement, the country also witnessed certain political and social upheavals such as the riots of 1915; and the birth of the nationalist and the socialist movements. Yet these movements did not inspire any radicalism in the painters of either the revivalist or the modern school.

Perhaps a little speculation can be permitted at this stage. The painters of the revivalist school and the modernists of the "43 Group" may have been either unaware of, or else excluded from their minds, any concern for the remarkable renaissance in painting that was at that time taking place in Mexico, where the writer and philosopher politician Jose Vasconcelos, during his tenure of office from 1921-24 at the Minister of Education, was able to implement "a far reaching programme which put art, aesthetic education and creativity at the peak of human achievement" and was able to achieve spectacular success in the field of painting by commissioning certain daring painters like Orozco, Riviera, and Sequiros to paint murals depicting the history, the nationalist struggle, and the life of the people of Mexico. The art historian Helen Gardner in her book, *Art through the Ages* considers the work of these artists as "the most exciting painting in the Americas ... an authentic national art ... strong in social significance and of the highest aesthetic quality."

Of the painters who by their individual example have had an impact on the young generation of artists working today, mention can be made of the academic painters such as A C G S Amerasekera and his son, Douglas; J D A Perera, David Painter and Stanley Abesinghe, who were influential Principals of the government school of Fine Arts; and the painters of the "43 Group" who have already been refereed to.

The Contemporary Situation

Today the work of the Sri Lankan painters of the present generation, reflect in varying degrees the three categories of 20th Century Sri Lankan art discussed earlier. The Academic style continues to be popular, but its possibilities which can restore an element of grandeur to the art of painting are hardly exploited. Revivalists too are yet in evidence, and are rendering a service in keeping alive the ancient and medieval styles, although there is an absence of new work on the scale of the modern Kelaniya murals. By far the great majority of today's artists are the inheritors of the legacy bequeathed to the country by the "43 Group". But whereas the enlightened painters of this group did not seek to establish *in toto* the modern but alien style of 20th Century Europe and sought to revitalize Sri Lankan art by introducing new ideas and forms; the majority of painters today appear to have succumbed rather tamely to the Euro-American manner of Abstract Art with a concern for amorphous form and textural effects with sometimes, a semblance of some recognizable shapes. Such works are extremely popular and are colourful and cleverly rendered. E H Gombrich, speaking of the abstract painter Kadinsky in his book, *Meditations on a Hobby Horse*, comments thus: "When I seriously compare my reactions to the best abstract canvas with some works of great music it fades into the sphere of the merely decorative." Gombrich's remark may well apply to much of the abstract work in vogue today when the 18th sculptor Falconet was faced with the prestigious position that antiquity enjoyed at the time, he pleaded "that we may be allowed, before genuflecting to consider the God." Modern art and its abstract variety in particular seems today to be enjoying the status of God. But its time that we consider this twentieth century phenomenon when that century is drawing to a close, and ask ourselves whether we should continue to genuflect in its presence any further.

Modern art, for well nigh a century has exerted a tremendous influence on painting in Sri Lanka. It cannot be denied that it has given fresh energy to, and revitalized the island's painting particularly in the second half of this century with the lead given by the "43 Group" of painters. However there is a need today to evaluate afresh the Euro-American centered field of modern art, closely scrutinizing it to assess whether this art and its ideas are adequate to satisfy the aesthetic needs of the Sri Lankan ethos. It is said that "the currency of art is debased if it robbed of its national ore." If that is so, a fresh search for this life-giving substance has to be made in our indigenous arts; in our classical and medieval traditions of Buddhists and Hindu art of the region; in the marvellously luminous miniature paintings of the Indo-Persian schools, and even in the national traditions further afield. There is again a need to bring back humanism and a concern for form rather than mere style if we are to see once again paintings of a richness and grandeur that were inspired by the great religions and ideologies.

PART III
WOMEN IN SOCIETY

A DIFFERENT VOICE: WOMEN WRITING IN BANGLADESH

Roushan Jahan

Introduction

A quarter-century has passed since the emergence of Bangladesh as a sovereign country. The war of liberation was a water-shed in all the major areas of national life. "Materializing the dreams and promises of 1971" and "upholding the spirit of the war of liberation", still remain the most resonant emotive appeal in the socio-political arena. The promise of the establishment of a secular democratic society based on the principles of economic and social justice, freedom from material want and cultural repression is still to be fulfilled. The last two decades have seen the launching of many organized efforts, initiated by concerned citizens for realization of the vision of preferred future. Some of the efforts focussed on specific issues and arenas of social life, some others tried to address the problems in a holistic and integrated manner. A notable feature of such efforts is the active participation of women in increasing number over time.

The increasing number and visibility of women are often seen as recent phenomena but women's activism is not new in Bangladesh. That gender, along with class and location, determines to a large extent, a person's access to and control over developmental opportunities, social resources and services was a well-known though seldom acted-upon fact. Despite constitutional guarantee of equal rights to all citizens, and provision for special measures for women and other disadvantaged sectors, national statistics shows glaring disparities between the position of male-female, rich-poor and rural-urban population. In addition, the disruptive and tragic potentials of the religious-communal and ethnic divides have been demonstrated very clearly in recent years particularly in the riots following the demo-Lition of the Babri mosque in Ayodhya and the protracted unrest in the Chittagong Hill tracts. Though as a group, women have been primarily identified by their gender and, consequently, gender-oppression has been their immediate deep concern, they were also aware that men, as well as women are victims of many types of oppression. In recent years, this realization has deepened as feminist research has brought to attention the linkage between the over-arching structures of oppression operating at various levels and the mechanisms which support them. The efforts, launched by women activists and researchers, to mobilize popular opinion and raise social awareness for social transformation through undermining the oppressive structures have been considerably strengthened by the incisive insights and passionate protest against injustice provided by women creative authors.

Here I propose to discuss briefly the different dimensions and perspectives which characterise recent writings by women: themes they prefer; the difference in world-view, their attitude to the prevalent gender-ideology, literary conventions and stereotypes; their awareness of the wider context in which they are located and the quest for identity which may or may not inform their work. Of the various literary forms, I would focus on poetry and fiction only.

As this is intended to be an opening statement on the subject in a regional dialogue no comprehensive description or analysis is attempted here. As the participants belong to various disciplines, I have tried to limit the use of jargons.

Women in Bangla Literature: Major Trends in Representation and Participation

Legacy of the Past: Conventions and Stereotypes

Representation of women in literature and the extent of their participation as writers (active agents) and readers (consumers) are closely related to their situation and position in a given society and culture especially informal education. In the pre-British period, social cultural values sanctioned segregation of the sexes, imposed strict gender division of labor and fostered a systematic bias of male supremacy. Women's biological role, defined in terms of reproduction and social functions associated with reproduction and nurturance was emphasized. As the bearer of the seed, and the carrier of the line women were held to be sexually vulnerable, needing to be jealously guarded from the lust of strangers. Chastity and modesty in women were valued at a premium and early marriage was perceived as the best strategy for providing "symbolic shelter" to young girls.

Several mechanisms and institutions maintained male dominance. The major one was the propagation of the ideology through sanctions by religious texts. Both Islamic and Hindu traditions maintained clearly that men and women were not only biologically different but that men were superior to women. The other mechanisms and institutions for maintaining male supremacy through domestication of women and strict control over their mobility, sexuality, and labor were: sex role stereotyping during childhood, socialization, gender division of work, segregation of the sexes in space (private and public) and differential allocation of resources and opportunities. Formal education was perceived to be non relevant for women's role in life which was to provide unpaid labor for the family and to ensure the supply (by bearing and rearing children) of future unpaid labor. As a consequence of this denial of education access to formal, very few women writers emerged at this time in Bengal.

Poetry was the major literary form preferred by the Bengali authors of this period. Poetical works, written by (mostly) men, for a largely male audience, described the emotions and deeds of men in love and war. The poets, both Hindu and Muslim, were deeply influenced by the aesthetic theory (Rasa Shastra) expounded in Sanskrit literature. Themes were borrowed directly from the Hindu epics, the Ramayana and the Mahabharata, which were translated in Bengali during this period. Even when the themes were not directly borrowed, the character of the hero and the heroine (*nayak* and *nayika*) were cast in the mould prescribed by Sanskrit literary convention.

The two types of heroines, presented in Sanskrit literature reflected the deep rooted male ambivalence towards women in a patriarchal society. The ancient Hindu myth of *Shree* (Lakshmi), the great mother goddess and *Urvashi*, the celestial dancer, rising out of the churning primordial ocean clearly sets the antithesis. *Lakshmi*, the ideal wife, symbol of fulfillment and plenty (female sexuality under male control and within the bounds of marriage) and *Urvashi*, the ideal courtesan, symbol of beauty and unrestrained gaiety (female sexuality beyond male control and outside marriage) — continued to be projected by Bengali poets even in this century as archetypes of women.

Their literary incarnations were: (a) Sita, the heroine of the Ramayana, the ideal Hindu *Kulastri* (woman of good family) whose devotion to husband, chastity, modesty and fortitude were extolled through the centuries for girls to emulate and (b) Vasantasena, the ideal *Ganika* (courtesan) the heroine of the play *Mirccha Katika* (the Clay Cart), the prototype of the 'fallen' girl with the golden heart, also portrayed endlessly by the future authors for young girls to take heed from example.

At first glance the two types seem to typify the two poles of a woman's existence when facing a pre set pattern (a) conformity to the norms set by the prevalent gender — ideology, and (b) rebellion against them. However, it is important to remember that patriarchal society itself recognized the need for the existence and maintenance of both types of women to serve specific male needs. Even the courtesan, for all the apparent freedom of sexual mobility and choice, was subject to a set of rigidly defined social customs. In fact, society seldom allowed women any space outside the confines of these moulds. Literature, the mouthpiece of the patriarchy, like the rest of the cultural apparatus, propagated that acceptance was the natural *dharma* of a woman, not rebellion. The heroines, presented by male authors of this period, thus, exhibit very little conflict within themselves. Even Radha, the celebrated heroine of the *Vaishnava Padabali* (lyric poems written by the poets of vaish nava sect such as Chandi dasa etc.), who dared to love Krishna outside the bonds of marriage, is no social rebel. While bitterly complaining about the cruelty of the social norms which separate her from Krishna and the condemnation by her in laws, she is never seen to raise any serious questions about the validity of such norms nor does she reject them. Similarly, the heroines of the popular Mymensingh Gitikas (ballads on secular love written by poets belonging to Mymensingh region), such as Mahua or Molua face crises quite bravely, but submit to the will of their lovers/husband's unquestioningly.

The advent of the colonial British, bearers of an alien culture and the sweeping reforms in the political, economic and cultural arena introduced by them caused a crisis of identity in both Hindu and Muslim Bengalis. Rapid changes in the wider context resulting from macro-processes of modernization, urbanization, industrialization, introduction of technology, exposure to the literature, culture and ideas of the West and other countries, introduction of universal primary education — all these generated considerable social analysis and examination/assessment of the existing social structures and institutions and as well as cultural traditions and customs, regarding both private and public life. Public discourse, including creative writing, in the nineteenth and early twentieth century, abounded in serious questioning of and protests against the unequal power relation and systematic oppressions stemming from hierarchies based on class, caste, gender, ethnicity, religion, and other socio political divides. Women's unequal situation and position in the family and the society appeared as a grave social issue. Alleviation of their situation became a priority agenda of social reform especially among the educated Hindus and Brahmos. Relaxation of purdah and access to formal education not only increased women's visibility but also gave them the exposure and training to analyze their own unequal and inferior position and the mechanisms which conditioned this inequality. They also had the opportunity to articulate their own thoughts and views,. thus complementing the representation made by men so long.

Two aspects of the response to Bengali identity crisis and woman question are note worthy. Firstly, though the Hindus responded earlier and the Muslim response came much later, there was a remarkable similarity in the pattern of response and attitude. In both the communities, a prolonged debate ensued between 'traditionalists, who urged the communities to cling to traditional values and customs and the modernists, who urged adaptation and reforms to suit the needs of modern times. Over time, the modernists gained ground. Secondly, though the modernists were in favour of women's participation in formal education, the major motivation for this education was to keep the traditional notion of 'womanhood' intact and to enable women to perform better as 'appropriate' wives and mothers in a modern household.

The major poets of the early twentieth century, Rabindranath Tagore and Kazi Nazrul Islam were imbued with a strong liberal humanism and protested against the many oppression unleashed by systems of inequalities based on imperialism, class, caste and gender. Patriotism, made strong by the political repression of the colonial rulers, along with romantic love for the beloved also appeared as dominant themes of many of the songs written by them which inspired the political activists. Despite such sensitivities, it should be noted that both these poets, as well as those who followed them in the later decades, still clung to the time honored image of the beloved cast in the patriarchal mould. The few women poets, all minor literary figures, were strongly influenced by the dominant diction.

Fiction in the form of novels and short stories written in prose also appeared in the nineteenth century Bengal. It gained popularity very rapidly. Overtime, the major writers have shown an increasing awareness of the conflicts and tensions inherent in gender relations both within marriage and outside marriage. Tagore and Sharatchandra had drawn very sensitive portraits of women in transition, torn between the pressure to conform with the norms imposed by society and rebellion against them. However, they and other contemporary male authors seemed to have accepted the centrality of marriage in a woman's life and motherhood as the major avenue of fulfillment for women. Women authors of the time such as Swarna Kumari Devi, Shailobala Ghoshjaya Anurupa Devi etc., while more critical about the double standard of sexuality and social restrictions on women's mobility and choice, also tended to reflect the same attitude toward marriage, love and motherhood as crucial to women's self fulfillment. Only Rokeya Sakhawat Hossain, the first and foremost feminist of Muslim Bengal, had the heroine of her novel *Padmaraga* declare that marriage is not the ultimate goal of a woman's life.

In 1947, British Bengal was divided in two provinces — East Pakistan and West Bengal belonging to two different states. In the next two decades the writers in east Pakistan were greatly influenced by their immediate socio-political context and responded to that. The repressions of a dictatorial regime, the crisis of democracy, the cultural impositions in the name of national integration, the tension between the religious and cultural-ethnic identity — all these informed their writings. But gender stereotypes still continued to haunt them. The face of the beloved in poetry and the heroines portrayed by the writers of fiction on the whole presented the traditional stereotypes.

Contemporary Poetry and Women in Bangladesh

Poetry is still the most popular literary form of self-expression. The major themes are: love, patriotic struggle, protest against social and political repression and economic exploitation, dehumanization of social environment and the alienation of individuals. The predominant voice is urban, educated middle class male.

The priority attached to protest originates from the 'left' orientation of our major poets, most of whom are the products of the 'radical' 60s and early 70s, a time of political activism against repressive and non-democratic regimes. Some scholars have pointed to the fact that many of the effective slogans used in the anti-autocracy movement during the 1980s come from poems written by such poets as Sikandar Abu Zafar, Shamsur Rahman, Nirmalendu Gun.

Indeed, *love* for persons (a woman) and the country as themes made intensely personal poems accessible to a great number of people. The existing socio-political repressive context also elicited instant response.

Fusion between the two muses — the beloved and the mother land-further strengthened the appeal to the predominantly male readers. The archetypal image shaped by the enduring myth of the 'good woman', a self-sacrificing, patient, devoted nurturer, is thus presented in new but familiar, idealized and sentimental forms.

Women poets, on the other hand, of necessity rejected the idealized and sentimental image of the beloved. The poems of Taslima Nasreen, Ruby Rahman and others refute the passive stereotype of women in love. Frank expression of women's sexuality, longing for shared intimacy, absence of guilt and false modesty mark their confessions of love and add a new tone.

Taslima Nasreen's satirical attack on patriarchal attitudes to women and gender — stereotype obviously is the most notable point of departure in 'protest' poetry. Earlier Bengali poets such as Tagore, Nazrul have written poems protesting gender-oppression and advocating women's entitlement to human dignity and personhood. But none had demonstrated like Taslima a passionate fury born of a deeply-felt wound. Her rejection of patriarchy and gender-discriminatory religion is direct and unhesitant. In one of her poems with ease and well chosen images she reduces the mighty male of the species to an insect, capable of causing only minor irritation and annoyance but no permanent damage to a woman's self-worth. At the same time her poems resonate with the loneliness of one who has chosen the road less travelled. It is easy to brand Taslima as a man-hater but that would be too simplistic. She detests the stereotypical male chauvinist who has no saving grace and articulates this in a telling manner in her poems.

Contemporary Fiction and Women in Bangladesh

Themes which recur in current fiction are: changing way of life and social institutions, i.e., the family, the work place, neighbourhood and the wider society; crises in the wider context impinging on the life of individuals and their struggle to cope with such crises. Especially emphasized are: dehumanization of social environments, break-up of family and erosion of joint-family values, unemployment, wide-spread corruption and violence which adversely affect the quality of life in the urban areas. Confusion, pessimism and nostalgia for things past (lost Eden) are the dominant mood characterizing the present-day fiction. Those written by men, are 'male-centred', focusing on a man's sense of alienation, lack of communication within marriage and family life.

The rural people and rural life are often depicted in stereotypes: ruthless, exploitative money-lenders and rich landholders *vis-a-vis* simple, uncomplicated people with limited aspirations struggling against them. There are exceptions. For instance Hasan Azizul Haq and Akhtar uzzaman Ilias depict the stark reality and multiple complexity of rural and urban life.

While some argue that the urban alienation is contrived because many authors still have rural roots one feels that for many, a distance has set in and the present reality of urban life supersedes the remembered rural past which partly contributes to the flat and non-realistic representation of rural life. Even less realistic perhaps is the representation of women.

The gender stereotype lingers on. The two faces of Eve, the benevolent and malevolent aspects of the great Goddess still persists. A popular motif is the disruption of the conjugal routine by the presence of another woman or man (the eternal triangle) externalizing the aggression and hostility, the growing apart and frequent coming together, still reminiscent of the novels of fifty years ago. The mother is still idealized and recalled with nostalgia. The bad woman, as a non-caring, greedy, selfish and often empty-headed, wife remains. In many novels, she is a shadow, not worthy of a fully developed portrait.

The obverse side of the coin is seen in novels written by women. The protagonists are women, laying bare the many layers of their selves. Even the apparent contradictions characterizing women depicted by male authors as manifestations of women's "natural" irrationality, are shown by the women authors to be logical outcomes of the circumstances in which women are placed. The protest against male oppression and rejection of patriarchal values and norms within marriage and family manifest in various ways in the novels and short stories written by the women authors, who had started writing in the 50s and 60s and are still continuing to write. Rabeya Khatun, Razia Khan, Dilara Hashem, Rizia Rahman,

Makbula Manzoor and other women have contributed significantly in projecting the image of life and society through women's perspective. Younger authors such as Taslima Nasreen and Nasreen Jahan have been notably bold in their treatment of issues related to gender-roles and relations and women's sexuality.

Thus in Taslima's *Shodh* (Revenge) the hostility and extreme desire for revenge drives an oppressed young woman to seduce a young man and have his child-only to foist the baby on her husband and his family. The husband who at one time compelled the woman to have an abortion because of baseless doubts about paternity and denied her the right to have a child is thus completely tricked from the real control over the wife's fertility and sexuality. Perverse over-drive for male control is countered by an equally perverse female hostility. The housewife who has neither a viable option to end her marriage nor any normal and recognized channel for self-assertion, nevertheless, thwarts the male control over her sexuality and fertility, albeit in a perverse fashion. A grim warning, surely, to male chauvinists.

Nasreen Jahan's *Urukku* (Flying 1993) depicts the struggles of a lower-middle class young woman who divorces her husband when his lack of sensitivity and routine sexual assaults become unbearable to her. The rejection and lack of support by her own blood kins; the harassment at the work place, her yearning to resume painting and her refusal to give in to the entreaties of her husband for re-marriage — are drawn with great insight. Her strengths and weaknesses — Jealousy of her good-looking sister who got male attention and mother's preference; her ambivalent feelings about motherhood, guilt and longing for the child she had lost; her courage in choosing not to terminate the pregnancy which resulted from her former husband's taking advantage of her are drawn with fine details. At the end of the novel we find her divested of illusions, reaching within herself to draw upon the inner reserves of self, getting ready to continue on the difficult journey of self-fulfillment, through motherhood and a career she has chosen freely. Economic self reliance and a survival network outside the claustrophobic conjugal and natal family are shown as significant conditions for a woman's liberation from oppression.

Protest against Political Repression and Social Injustice

Male authors writing about the language movement of 1952, the popular uprising against the repressive army regime in 1969, above all the war for liberation in 1971, generally focus on middle-class student volunteer freedom fighters and army officials. Though the people were the real heroes, their stories are still untold. With a few exception, the story line resembles classic Hollywood "Westerns". Drawn in black and white, it is rendered as a fight between the hero (freedom-fighter) and the villain (Pakistani army official/Razakar).

Women and rural people are shadowy, stereotype, flat. Women are shown mostly wringing their hands, waiting to be rescued by the hero from a fate worse than death (rape). In some cases, they are victims of atrocities, waiting to be rehabilitated and in others, they are the long-suffering fiances of the freedom fighters waiting patiently for the return of the hero. The mothers and sisters, ministering angels, are also present in many novels, as inspirational figures.

Women writers have just started to reject this male-centred history by writing 'her story'. Selina Hossain's *Apna Mase Harina Bairi* written in 1980 (the Plumed Peacock, 1983) for instance tells the story of Kanupada, a poor poet who yearns to establish the dignity of the vernacular at the royal court of medieval Bengal, where Sanskrit, the official language is used. His unconventional stand draws the anger of the Brahmin minister who imprisons him. Two women, Shaboree, the beautiful, dependent and devoted wife, whose aim in life is to obey and please Kanu and Dombee, the dancing-girl, who is free, lively and self-reliant, inspire Kanu to sing and closely resemble the classical stereotypes of Lakshmi and Urvashi. However the author deviates from the stereotype in startling ways. The Dombee kills the minister's nephew who pesters her with unwelcome attentions and bravely face death. Shaboree, who patiently sheds tears and waits for Kanu's return from prison very untypically joins the mass-uprising at the end of the story, like some medieval Ila Mitra of the Tebhaga Movement fame. It is interesting to note how the woman author neatly reassigns roles and flouts the conventions about gender-stereotypes in this (thinly veiled) retelling of the story of the 1952 movement for establishment of Bengali as state language by situating it in the medieval setting.

No matter which theme is chosen, the novels and short stories written by women authors underscore the basic humanness and personhood of women. They demonstrate the contrived and male-imposed nature of the exaggerated gender-division and reject the patriarchal notions about the 'masculine and the feminine' nature. Above all, they advocate very convincingly the obsoleteness of the traditional terms and conditions of marriage, the untenability of social expectations from women to conform to gender-norms at all costs and the need for new ground rules for gender relations and the basic social institutions and structures.

Conclusion

In 1905, Rokeya Sakhawat Hossain, the first and foremost feminist of Muslim Bengal, dreamed of empowering women in her feminist utopian story (Sultana's Dream) by a simple reversal of gender roles, putting men in seclusion and letting women take charge of the public sphere. For the inheritors of Rokeya's dream of women's empowerment, the task is complex and difficult. While the activists have to think of strategies for an alternate paradigm of development based on participatory politics, egalitarian distribution of social resources, free expression of pluralistic culture and non-hierarchical gender relations in the family, community and state, they would depend heavily on the women writers to continue a counter-discourse for raising social awareness. Reluctance of the dominant male to give up privileges which they have enjoyed unfairly on the grounds of gender; increasing hostility from the fundamentalists and reactionary forces towards the advocates of secularism, pluralism and freedom of expression; continued intrusion of the state to limit the basic rights of individuals are serious challenges. Fortunately, the recent works of Bangladeshi women writers indicate their willingness to face such challenges. They have already rejected the restraining images and moulds created by the dominant male and are fashioning their own idiom for self expression, informed by their own innermost feelings, desires, knowledge and world-view.

The articulation of their vision, combined with the struggles of the activists to realize it, has made an impact on Bangladeshi social consciousness and women's own identity and self-image. Intensely personal though the act of creative writing is, it is also an act with a deep social meaning. Hopefully, women writers would continue to remain connected with and committed to the ideals of a holistic development of the self and the society to which they belong.

Contemporary South Asian Art and Women

Nazrul Islam

The artists at all times and in all places have been concerned with the nature of women (as much as, or even more than, the nature of men). The artists of the South-Asian sub-continental region have similarly found women and their life an absorbing subject for the expression of their creative activities. Artists have depicted women, as women, at work, at play, in love, in nature, as women and their ideas, women in their conflicts and also women as goddesses. In the contemporary situation, the last named theme (women as goddesses) is nearly irrelevant, while the other themes persist. The contemporary modern artists in South Asia have also pursued the above themes while depicting women. In very recent times, one of the most famous of the South Asian artists, M.F. Hussain, landed in serious trouble for having drawn sketches of a Hindu goddess in the nude. Had he been an artist of the 10th century and sculpted a figure of the deity he would probably have no problem. However, the artist's own religious identity would perhaps still cause a problem. Art and artists, even today, seem to have caste and creed. In any case, our topic of discussion in this paper is women in contemporary South Asian Art, particularly with reference to such issues as (i) women in society, (ii) social justice and human rights and (iii) fundamentalism and communalism.

By the term contemporary art, we will confine ourselves to the last five decades, meaning post-independence or post-colonial period.

However, some references may go beyond 1947. We will also confine ourselves to contemporary "modern" art rather than discuss "traditional" or "folk arts". Our discussion is also limited to the arts of Bangladesh, Nepal, India, Pakistan and Sri Lanka, five of the seven South Asian countries participating in the CPD Dialogue. (In the latest Asian Art Biennial Bangladesh 1995, artists of Bhutan also assumed a westernised modernistic posture and depicted women and the girl child in their work. But Bhutanese contemporary artists in general like to adhere to traditional styles. The artists of the Maldives have not been participating in the Asian Biennial for some time and we have no clear idea about their recent artistic activities. Until the late eighties, they were, however, portraying women in a realistic manner. These were women at leisurely work or women in love).

It is not very easy to find expression of all three themes of the dialogue in the contemporary arts of the region. For example, fundamentalism and communalism have found little portrayal in the artistic works of major artists of South Asia. One may also have to search hard to find evidence of works on social justice and human rights. However, examples of works under the theme of "women in society" may not be very difficult to get, as the theme addresses a much broader subject.

Fundamentalism and Communalism

Some of the leading South Asian contemporary modern artists have held politically quite radical views and stood against fundamentalism and communalism. In Bangladesh, Quamrul Hasan's name is remembered with reverence in this context. He participated in many anti-fundamentalist agitations, but we do not find serious works of art by him on the theme. Although many brutal incidents have taken place in Bangladesh in which women became victim of fundamentalists' verdicts. Like the case of Noorjahan, who ultimately had to commit suicide because of fundamentalist persecution, has moved few artists. Dilara Begum Jolly, a young female artist, is an exception. Her painting "Noor Jahan" is a statement against fundamentalism. Jolly has also been depicting violence against women in general in a rather surrealistic manner. She was chosen for an honourable mention in the twelfth national exhibition of art last December (1996) for her painting "Violence-3". In this work the central focus of violence is a woman.

In India, as has been mentioned earlier, an artist of the eminence of M.F. Hussain himself became victim of fundamentalist and communal attack, not for standing against fundamentalism or communalism, but for depicting goddess Saraswati in a rather unorthodox manner. Although he made these sketches many years ago, the reaction from fundamentalists came only recently. Hussain has depicted more worldly women, both celebrities and ordinary. His attitude is not so much political as it is social or simply artistic.

Although fundamentalism is a very strong force (getting even stronger) in Pakistan, there is very little evidence in art showing protest against this force. None of the 26 illustrations in the comprehensive volume on *Contemporary Art in Pakistan* by Marcella Nelson Sirhandi (Ferozsons, Lahore, 1992) show any such evidence, neither had the seven Asian Art shows in Dhaka since 1981 provided any example of artists rising against fundamentalism. Although the "Women Series" of Nahid Raza or works by other artists have placed women in the centre of their focus.

Despite the fact that Sri Lanka is tormented by ethnic or racial strifes, there is little sign of such disturbance in the art works of this country. The artists seem to be able to maintain a distance and remain calm.

Social Justice and Human Rights

The questions of social justice and human rights, political as these are, have attracted attention of many contemporary artists of the sub-continent but once again the depiction of these issues in their works have not been that plentiful.

Zainul Abedin, the pioneer of the modern art movement in Bangladesh, made his mark as an artist with his famous sketches on the 1943 Famine in Bengal. These sketches are poignant statement on the cruelty of colonial exploitation and social injustice. Many other artists of Calcutta at that time (Ramkinkar, Somnath Hore,

Chittaprasad, Sudhir Khastagir, Gobardhan Aash, Paritosh Sen, Gopen Roy, Bhobesh Sanyal, Sunimadhau Sen, etc.) have also depicted the famine scenes in their works and focused on the vulnerability of women in particular. But the sketches of Abedin have attained almost a symbolic status on social injustice through famine. It is interesting to note after over fifty years since the famine sketches how perceptively Abedin had recorded the plight of the women, the mother. She had not only to fend for herself, but also for the children, because the father, or the man, had abandoned the family, looking only after himself. Quamrul Hasan, the other most powerful and influential modern artist of Bangladesh, was also deeply concerned at the lack of social justice and human rights, particularly of women. Some of his post-liberation works, specially the large wood cut compositions of 1974, depicting the famine on the one hand and the vulgarity of the urban rich on the other, are strong statements on social inequality. Much younger artists of Dhaka, like Shishir Bhattacharya, Rokeya Sultana, Nilufar Chaman or Dilara Begum Jolly, have also satirized the predicament of women in an unequal society. Hundreds of thousands of women during the Bangladesh War of Liberation suffered violation of their human dignity and rights, and some artists have chosen such experiences as their subject matter.

Amrita Sher-Gil in India, Zubaida Agha in Pakistan or Novera Ahmed in Bangladesh were some of the pioneer women artists of the sub-continent with whom women received special attention. All three artists were thoroughly modern, Novera in sculpture and Sher-Gil and Agha in painting. Sher-Gil and Novera are particularly noteworthy as they chose ordinary women as the subject of their work (Lala Rukh Selim has made a thorough analysis of Novera's portrayal of women, in her paper in this dialogue).

Women in Society

Of the three themes, 'Women in Society' is more practically illustratable on the basis of their greater representation in works of modern art in South Asia.

Pioneer artists like Zainul Abedin, Quamrul Hasan or S.M. Sultan in Bangladesh, Abdur Rahman Chugtai, Shakir Ali or Zubaida Agha in Pakistan, Amrita Sher-Gil, Leela Mukherjee, M.F. Hussain, G. Surbramanium, Meera Mukherjee, Ganesh Pain, Sarbari Roy Chowdhury and many others in India, George Keyt, JDA Perera or Stanley Abesinghe, Madapatha Dhamasera Thera and ALD Sirisena in Sri Lanka, and artists in Nepal have seen women in various strata of their respective society. Chugtai only placed women in high society, as a contrast, Zainul, Quamrul and Sultan were more engaged in depicting the life of ordinary women or working women, Hussain chose both famous personalities like Mother Teresa, Indira Ghandi and more recently even film actress Madhuri Dixit to symbolize womanhood. Amrita Sher-Gil had changed the attitude towards women in Indian art by addressing ordinary village women.

In the contemporary modern art of Bangladesh it was Shahabuddin who took a lead in depicting political and social leaders, both dead and living. Shahabuddin was bold enough to portray Bangabandhu Sheikh Mujibur Rahman during the eighties when it was indeed a taboo to do so. Other artists came forward only after Sheikh Hasina became the Prime Minister. Shahabuddin is also the pioneer in portraying great women of Bangladesh in his canvas. He depicted Sufia Kamal, Jahanara Imam and Sheikh Hasina in his recent works. There are not many other artists who chose to do the same.

Most of the young artists of Bangladesh, including women artists, are more down to earth in the selection of their subject matters, but quite surreal, post-modern and highly satirical in style of depiction. On the other hand, some very senior painters (like Mortuza Basheer) of Bangladesh, have found greater interest in the portrayal of middle class urban women in cosmetic attire in a more romantic semi-realistic style. Sensuality and even eroticism also pervade in the works of young artists, mostly males, but also females, while depicting women. Women in love, or men and women making love, are also not rare scenes. At the same time the dignity of women, women as contributors to economic productivity, as symbol of fertility, of motherhood, continue to be depicted in art.

We might conclude by noting that the artists of the South-Asian subcontinent have been fairly conscious of the socio-political status of women in the society but have normally not taken much of a radical stand in depicting their situation in works of art. However, at least in Bangladesh, modern painting has remained very secular in content all along.

WOMEN IN THE CONTEMPORARY ART WORLD OF BANGLADESH: IMAGES AND REALITY

Lala Rukh Selim

The art of this region has a long and wonderful past. As part of the sub-continent, Bengal shared various trends in art that developed and flourished in the rest of India. Regional distinction also found expression in the arts of Bengal at different times with the changing socio-political context.

As in the rest of the world, the changing socio-economic status of women has found expression in the arts of this land. Women as bearers of life, symbols of fertility, mysterious and powerful beings have from the very beginning fascinated, perplexed and overawed men. Worship of the fertility of nature, on which mankind depended, developed and fertility itself has been embodied in the form of the pregnant woman, the mother goddess. With the advent of civilization and the changing cultures and values, women have always featured in art as society, and in most cases, patriarchal society has chosen to depict them. Role of women in the 'high' arts has always been determined by men while the folk or popular arts have been relatively less restricted as they have sometimes been practised by womenfolk themselves and have shown the women's perspective in different cultures. This same pattern weaves the fabric of our own art world.

The advent of Islam in Bengal brought about a break with the past tradition. Islam frowned upon the figure in art. Culture became compartmentalized into Muslim and non-Muslim culture. Things became further complicated with the advent of the British who, for a beginning, placed very little value in the wealth of art teeming in this part of the world. They set up their own art institutes to train people not to be artists but to learn to create objects to glorify and further consolidate the British empire. Thus, the fine arts developed, as in all cultures, from ritualistic, religious or political needs. With the British academic schools that were set-up in different parts of the sub-continent the artist community came into contact with their highly formalised, rigid schooling. These academies were rarely attended by Muslims from our parts as Islam is intolerant of art and women dabbling in this field was out of the question. Thus women have only recently stepped into the arena of the 'high' or fine arts. We see no women among the first generation of artists who laid the foundation of the modern art movement of Bangladesh. We hear of no women students studying in the Govt. School of Arts, Calcutta, parallel to Zainul Abedin, Quamrul Hasan, Shafiuddin Ahmed or S.M. Sultan, who were the pioneers of modern Bangladeshi art.

With the partition of Bengal and the birth of Pakistan the issues of national identity and integrity became further disjointed. Were we Muslims first or Bengalees first? Which roots should we recognize and nurture? Religious values were strictly imposed to bind East and West Pakistan together where almost no other common boundaries existed.

The Government Institute of Arts was established in Dhaka in 1948 after the partition of Bengal. Zainul Abedin was instrumental behind the founding of the institute. The first batch of female students joined it in 1954. They were Tahera Quayyum, Rawshan Ara Amin, Moeena Iqbal and Hasina Zaman Minu.[1] It is to be surmised that they were not ordinary girls from ordinary families. They had the courage to stand up to being regarded from under raised eyebrows which must have followed them around in those conservative times. However they could not go on to become successful artists. We have examples of women getting admitted to

[1] Vide, Nasim Ahmed Nadvi, "Introduction", *She A Group Art Exhibition,* Dhaka 1994.

leave the course unfinished and some who actually completed the course never to put their training to any creative use. Somehow the bondage of marriage, family, children and art have not proven a good combination at least for women. Social pressure and the duties and obligations of the family can never be conducive to the concentration, dedication and above all else, the constant practice that is a must for the creative process to work. The creative process requires the harmony of vision, intuition and execution without which true art cannot be created. For men it is allowable that they found a family, earn the bread and remain in the position of the remote outsider from other family duties. Not so for women. Even today the economically independent woman is more harassed then in the past with the effort to synthesize her different worlds of the home, the workplace and at the same time tapping her creativity for the flow of ART.

It is interesting to note that the first woman to leave her mark in the modern art movement of Bangladesh was a social outsider, Novera Ahmed. Novera Ahmed's appearance in the art scene of Bangladesh was not the culmination of social events which made the appearance of a woman artist inevitable or acceptable. She was more like a comet which suddenly appears lighting the sky with blinding light to vanish without a trace. She had no antecedents and left no immediate predecessors. She created a turmoil in her times so that whoever who was in any way connected with cultural matters knew of her presence. Her presence was no common presence! "... [Novera] appeared as an apparition, a spectre. On closer view, it was a small, intense woman, dressed severely in black, with a bead necklace around her neck and no other ornament, penetrating eyes and a mysterious mien, that reminded one of the priestess of a long forgotten cult, a votaress in a temple."[2] These are the words of Abdus Salam editor of "Pakistan Observer" written in the catalogue printed for the first exhibition of sculptures in this country by Novera in 1960.

Novera was born in the early 1930's in a culturally inclined family. She learnt to sing and dance and grew up watching her mother make

[2] Vide, Abdus Salam, "A Spirit Devoted to Art", *Inner Gaze, Sculptures of Novera Ahmed*, Dacca, 1960.

clay models. This probably dictated the decidedly 'unfeminine' calling she chose in life. As a young woman she was married off to an eligible suitor but she rebelled against the marriage to run away to her elder sister who lived in London. She enroled in the Camberwell School of Arts and Crafts in London to study sculpture under Sir Jacob Epstein and chose to come back to former East Pakistan after she finished her course. In Dhaka she lived alone, kept no contact with her relatives to protect her independence and commenced her solitary battle to create sculpture in a land where it was totally new territory, considered irreligious and unacceptable. It was she who created the first outdoor sculpture and the first frieze on the wall of a public edifice which alone should have given her a place as a forerunner in the field of art. In the words of Zainul Abedin in the catalogue of Novera's 1st exhibition, "In East Pakistan's art world, it was a minor revolution, when Novera Ahmed gave the city the first frieze on the wall of the Central Public Library in 1957 and then the first open air sculpture in 1958. We, the citizens of Dacca, have been living with this [Sic.] two magnificent work [Sic.] for [the] past few years. But I still think, we shall take generations to assess the impact of these two work [Sic.] in our art life."[3] Alas, Zainul Abedin's words have proven prophetic because even after almost forty years have elapsed we are still unable to correctly evaluate and acknowledge the historical and aesthetic significance of these two works and the body of works that Novera left behind in this city of Dhaka when she left it forever, disillusioned, rejected and probably disheartened. She had her dreams, the dreams of building a city enlivened with sculpture and other works of art to create citizens enlightened by them, "We must ignite among our people the spark of curiosity, about the inner visions, meanings and truths of life, which can come only by bringing art within the horizon of our city life."[4]

Apart from the challenge of establishing sculpture as an art form, creating her own language which would at the same time spring from the roots of her own culture, the whole process of coming to

---

[3] *Ibid*, Zainul Abedin, "Postscript".

[4] *Ibid*, S.M. Ali, "Inner Gaze".

terms with her medium must have been considerable for Novera. She who was used to working in an institute with all modern facilities of models, materials and technicalities, came to Dhaka to find it barren indeed in these areas. She remoulded her methods of execution and her forms to suit the conditions and materials that she had at hand and within a very short space of time successfully created her own language.

In Dhaka in those days of political fervour and activism she must also have been part of the surging nationalistic zeal which was born after the Language Movement of 1952. Novera chose to look eastward to her own tradition when she struggled to create her forms and images. Thus we find forms captured from the folk dolls of our region simplified, exaggerated and activated by her skilful analysis and her presence. Village dwellers were often her source of inspiration. Her work testifies to the struggle to combine her Western schooling with the spirit of national identity.

Even though she was a very individual artist and a very private person with her sculpture definitely created for herself alone, to give meaning to her existence, she was not unconscious of her social obligations as a responsible and conscious person. She was deeply involved in the planning of the Shaheed Minar, designing fountains and sculptures which never materialized.[5]

The fascinating part about Novera's work is the image of the woman. We see her generation of male artists struggling to combine the voluptuous sensuality of European females with a romanticizing of women so prevalent in our country. Stilted, suggestive scenes of rural women bathing in clinging drapery, at their toilet with comb or mirror, sniffing a bloom, etc. Women were resolutely kept out of the world of activity. Other than this the image of 'ma', motherhood, an eastern concept which is the saving grace that gives woman an elevated status in this part of the world, is the prevailing image. In Zainul Abedin's famous famine sketches we do see women as a part of the vast sea of suffering humanity devoid of sentimentality and all other western or eastern feminine attributes. Occasionally we even gaze into the face of a pensive woman in his paintings because

---

[5] Vide, "Novera Ahmed", *Art A Quarterly Journal*, January 1994, P. 8.

he was a compassionate and feeling person with a concern for people irrespective of sex. Yet the characteristic woman is definitely not one 'in action'.

Quamrul Hasan is a completely different matter choosing himself as the focus, all his women are his. Either his mother, wife or daughter. Devoid of individuality or feeling, they are created with the sole idea of pleasing others. These two major artists are mentioned here as examples of the female image in the eyes of male artists to compare with Novera's female images.

Novera Ahmed's work shows the female image in a totally different light from the eyes of men. Her female forms are not seen through the idealizing focus we notice in men. In her groups men and women are seen as units coming together to form a whole, to create a compositional design. What strikes me as a distinctive feature in Novera's work is her effort to go beyond the creation of superficial and pleasing forms. She wanted to peel her forms of all excesses to present her vision and her statement in meaningful, simple and original terms. This is no easy task because one has to rely on the truth of the concept much more than on the skill of the craftsmanship. She was definitely interested in presenting certain ideals and on occasion, reality. She had the driving force of her convictions and her total concentration on her art alone in her position as the eccentric outsider that gave her the power to relentlessly keep at her work and explore new territory with her inner gaze. When Novera created women in sculpture she stripped the images of all maudlin sentimentality to create forms of real women, stubborn, determined, with a frank eroticism such as we see in *The Long Wait*. Her mothers are not pretty but are strong and bold and struggling. Often they go beyond the realm of mere individual feeling to become symbols of mankind. As Mervyn Marshall of England said of this piece, "*The Long Wait* is a typical example of Novera's work. In this basic, primitive outline, one feels the longing and the despair the resignation and resolution of a whole people waiting for deliverance!"[6]

---

[6]Vide, Mervyn Marshall, "The Long Wait", *Inner Gaze, Sculptures of Novera Ahmed*, Dacca 1960.

Unfortunately enough the efforts of Novera have till now found very little appreciation in our art world and Zainul Abedin's words echo down through the years as the bitter truth. One questions oneself why is Novera forgotten? Would she have been allowed to sink from sight as she did if she had been a he? What happened to the '100 pieces'[7] of sculpture that finds mention in the 1960 catalogue of her exhibition? Why was she compelled to leave the country while many other artists (and many of lesser merit) found fame and social acclaim?

Novera's crimes were many. For a beginning she was a woman and a beautiful one at that and again she was born in the 1930's. She chose sculpture as her calling and not the better accepted painting. She was delightfully bohemian, unable to conform to any social norms and could not be measured by them. Her eccentricities were not pretensions to attract attention, they were actual demonstrations of her concept of life, how she wanted to be and was. She was not a successful public relations person. She was honest and she was what she was. What happened was that men were fascinated by her because she was beautiful and extraordinarily uninhibited in her relations. As a result when one talks about Novera with her contemporary males they speak at length on Novera as a personality but have very little to say of her work which seemed minor to them in comparison to her persona. Many wish to dismiss her work as the useless exercises of a flighty female. I may add that this has gone to the advantage of many who wish to be recognized as pioneers of areas which were already covered by Novera years ago! Thus the Novera phenomenon is resolutely a skeleton in the cupboard and she is a victim of sexism like many others. Her name is not to be mentioned in the academies that teach art in our country. Some of her '100 pieces' stand maimed and broken and some have only very recently been collected by the national Museum. If she had been a man would we not have eyed her eccentricities with tolerance and indeed glorified them as we do those of all our great men? We can only say that there is still time for us to look, analyze and record our history with reference to reality. With the vanishing act that Novera

[7] *Ibid*, S.M. Ali. "Inner Gaze".

performed in the 1960's we unfortunately lost the only woman in the field of art for years to come. Novera's generation of male artists returned home from abroad in the sixties armed with western aesthetic values and relentlessly set to battle often to set their roots in the air instead of into the earth and the Modern Art movement in Bangladesh was underway. Women artists struggled under-water never to properly reach the surface while the image of woman found a place in the arts as the object of romance, sentiment or fantasy of men. Only in the 1970's again do we see women as artists emerging as a tangible part of the art world, holding their own to some degree. This seems to be the actual fruit of social change and a change in the status of women. Such artists as Laila Monsur Nazlee, Masuma Khan, Farida Zaman, Naima Haque, Shamim Shikder, Sadhana Islam, etc., are artists who completed their studies in the institutes in the early 70's and are active as artists to this day. The first group show of women artists was by the "Group of Four" in 1974 which included works of Farida Zaman, Naima Haque, Shamim Shikder and Shadhana Islam. This is a landmark in our art world. These women struggled on and mostly went abroad to further their studies. Farida Zaman was the first ever woman artist to receive recognition from the government by being awarded the "Young Artists Award". This change in the position of our women artists was the fruit of our awareness as a people which had sharpened from the Language Movement of 1952 to the climax in the War of Liberation in 1971. It was the liberation of our beings as a total nation. Men and women struggled equally for freedom and nationalistic fervour overcame the confines of religious or social restrictions. It was the time when the nation had dreams and hopes and anything was deemed possible. To believe in the equality of men and women came to be considered a basic requirement for any progressive being.

From the 70's onwards women have become increasingly active in the art scenario of Bangladesh. The number of female students in the art institutes are increasing as are the number of teachers. Farida Zaman, Naima Haque, Shamim Shikder, Rowshan Haq Dipa, Nasreen Begum, Rokeya Sultana, Dilara Begum Jolly, Niloofar Chaman and others are well known in the art field as serious practising artists. Our women are receiving acclaim both at home and abroad. There is a strong participation of women in any national or international exhibition held in the country and they are active in all the different media. Group shows by women are also common fare nowadays. As in the rest of the world, women artists in Bangladesh are in focus now.

Women artists do not have to achieve the level of intensity and solitude that Novera Ahmed needed in her time to declare her individuality and freedom of spirit. They do not have to dress and make-up to look bizarre or shocking to announce and retain their existence and their faith in it as Novera did. Things are easier, on the whole.

With this loosening of boundaries we see certain changes transforming our art world, the emergence of new trends and a diversification of subject and style. In the wake of the footsteps of our women the feminine perspective and feminine value is added to art. It is no easy task to liberate the female image created by men, all our training, all the books on art and the visual materials that confronts us drums it into us. Yet the female image has come out of the stereotype into more fluid and 'real' forms as they are created by women themselves who are inside the spirit of the forms. This is not to say that all our women are engaged in creating art that is socially committed and feministic. There are many women who are practising non-figurative or non-representational art. Those who are doing representational art may not be dealing specifically with women's issues but since they are women their experiences and attitudes definitely find expression in their work and this is totally different from that of men. Women here are real beings, not figments of the imagination. There are some women who have consciously used their art to make social statements about the plight of women, statements against religious fundamentalism and repression. On the whole when one is confronted by the work of a group of women artists one is made quite conscious that women are thinking about themselves, for themselves.

To discuss a few examples we see in Laila Mansur Nazlee's work the image of women predominating mostly a social panorama where the claustrophobia of a woman's existence is the focus. Her women are active, flesh and blood persons depicted in different gestures.

Rowshan Haq Dipa has at times painted women who are obviously in difficulties and are unhappy. Strong and sensuous women hounded or overshadowed by men who look threatening, almost menacing. Dilara Begum Jolly is a frank feminist in her themes. Her paintings and prints show her in the role of a social critic. She has satirized and presented violence in society and very often violence against women in her work. Religious fundamentalism was her focus for a long time. For instance her *Noorjahan* is the expression of her personal agony and her feeling of solidarity with Noorjahan who was a village maiden buried to her waist and stoned by her villagers at the instigation of fundamentalists who had accused her of adultery. Noorjahan later committed suicide. Jolly's women are women with all their failings and strengths. She is no romantic and life is no dream in her impassioned creations. Niloofar Chaman's paintings are a world of fantasy, a gloomy, acid coloured world peopled by women, men and animals who are immensely cerebral and intensely bored, sad? Her men and women are almost indistinguishable and emerge as similar forms. Her works is quite unique. Her fantasies are symbolic depictions of what is often her outrage at what is happening around her. The phallic forms that she uses and her erotic imagery are derived from a female point of view. The frank eroticism in her images of humans, animals and plant life shows her individuality and a feminine perspective of sexuality. Rokeya Sultana who has been working on her *Madonna Series* for quite some time shows her Madonna in an urban setting, a woman with her child struggling against the crowd of adversities that afflict a working mother.

All in all, one is quite conscious of the fact that women are victims of social injustice and this comes across quite strongly in the work of a lot of our women. It is undeniable that the work of our women is as much overshadowed by the identity crisis as is our total art world which is looking for ways to synthesising its cultural and national identity while at the same time being international and individual with the overpowering influence of Western art movements gripping the very foundations of its modern art.

Considering the last 30 to 40 years I can only say that our women have definitely changed the climate of our art world with their presence. The female images that they create are charged with lived experience, strength and depth of feeling and the truth of their very existence enlivens them and gives them verity. Yet women are still only on the threshold of all that can be achieved. Just as art is not a discrete and unique phenomenon, separated from society, neither are artists. True genius may transcend all barriers but much strength and goodness may be lost in the process.

THE IMAGE OF WOMEN ON TV AND CINEMA

Sara Zaker

Nayeeka is the Bengali word for a female central lead played by the women actor in play or a feature film. The role played by the *Nayeeka* is essentially created by the man and the sexist connotation is deeply entrenched in the implications of the *Nayeeka*. Hardly are there plays of the television or feature films of the film industry of Bangladesh that does not feature the *Nayeeka* in the image that it connotes. This *Nayeeka* that the audience is continually exposed to is undoubtedly a very attractive figure and indeed to be emulated, as made obvious from the endorsement by playwrights through their continuous presence on screen. The image that she conjures up among the target audience however is aptly summed up in the undulating lines, the rosy cheeks and charcoal eyed drawings of the women from the showbiz on the rickshaw backs plying the roads and alleys of the country.

That, women are an unequal lot is accepted by all class, colour and creed of the world in various degrees of ire or consent.

That, media shapes human minds is also an universal truth. In today's world the power of mass media to communicate and educate the huge cross section of people stands beyond argument. What had once been the domain of commercial marketers has now been usurped by the politicians. As more people are getting access to the mass media of television and cinema, the "tube" and the "celluloid" areas becoming more and more dear to people who care to have a good share of voice and visual presence on them. Also, in this vastly illiterate world of ours the audio visual medium has a far greater impact than any other medium.

That, the women's unequal status *vis-a-vis* the man is a sociopolitical question, is a commonly shared notion by all right thinking people of the world.

Thus, if the lot of the women has to improve, a colossal job remains to be done in the rebuilding of her image through the mass media of television and cinema.

The Film Development Corporation was formed in 1950. Ever since its inception, the film industry has functioned as very good industrial enterprise. As it became more and more important to make the film commercially viable, the women in the films came to be used increasingly as a commodity. In the event where 'women' are hooks for commercial success, little can be excepted from the role played by them to change the status in society. Thus, the participation of women in commercial venture defeats the cause of the women and we can presume that it necessitates no further deliberation. Also, as instrument of social change, the cinema has lost its credibility ever since its reach has been overtaken by television. Cinema provides unadulterated entertainment to the masses, vast majority of whom are male. What is seen in the celluloid is a fantasy world and emulation is not the driving force. Thus cinema, as it stands today, is not so much an impediment in the reconstruction of the women's image in the way television is. Television's unique role in bringing social changes is now universally recognized. When speaking of building image, in the way stage is excluded as any mode reconstruct, cinema too may be excluded from the task of exacting the job.

Television had been homely media and on it's fringe when it started operating in the early sixties in Dhaka. In the beginning it was only in the capital, but soon it reached out to all corners of the country and even to across the boundaries to India by the mid seventies. This position changed further as more and more TV sets came into the middle class households. A phenomenal change was witnessed nineties with the mushroom growth of satellite dishes on roof tops and the webs of satellite cables that crisscrossed the sky soon after. Now when TV has overtaken the cinema in its reach and splendor the TV starts too now adorn the tin backs of the rickshaws on the Dhaka streets which hitherto had been exclusively dominated by the heroines of the tinsel world.

The subject of the discourse is the image of women. The important role of mass media is its power to create role models. Roles that are recreated by the respective target groups at empathy with them. It is widely believed that images built through the mass media create the mirror image in the society. Shakespeare had said that the job of the playwright was to hold a mirror onto nature. Obviously Shakespeare's concern was to improve the form of art. In the mean time of more than one or half a century from his age we have come to a situation in which whether or not we reflect "Life in Art" people will follow the Art or the likeness of it by represented in the electronic Art form of television.

In the light of the argument of this paper, that the continual presence of *Nayeeka* as the female lead defeats the cause of status change for the women, we may look closely into her aspect.

Nayeeka from the days of yore till date in Television or in Cinema, is the women lead who may be defined by the following attributes:

1. Young (preferable spanning the years eighteen through twenty five);
2. Beautiful and the criteria of fairness & attractive qualify the beauty;
3. Belonging to the middle class; and
4. Manoeuvreable.

As in literature and poetry, so also in drama, the women cast in this mould re-inforces the perception about the women in a way that it becomes 'ideal' role to follow. This is a tall order for the majority of women to achieve. At an individual level it creates stress for the women to fit into the category and at the social level the *Nayeeka's* position at the centre excludes all other women of the society from focus of attention. Thus any women who cannot meet the standards of *Nayeeka* in one less in her accomplishment, whatever her achievements may be otherwise. This creates a set back for the women, as in addition to her other efforts, more than necessary time is spent by her to make herself as close as possible to the *Nayeeka*.

In comparison, her counterpart man is better placed, for his attention is more concentrated on accomplishment as he himself defines it, and even if society defines it, it is not merely a superficial accomplishment that is modelled by the *Nayeeka*. This contribution of the ART and POETRY towards the IMAGE of women and mass marketed by media is so strongly embedded in our psyche that we are actually talking of a homogeneous job, if are to think about changing the practice altogether.

We cannot hope to remove the *Nayeeka* from the central focus of attention of "Business". However, we can well use this central position of the "woman" in media to the advantage of image reconstruction for the new woman.

Recommendations

The maturity is accompanied by confidence of facing the world, is a far more attractive and comfortable position to be in for the woman than blushing in her discomfort with the world. Thus maturity could be opted in place of innocence for the reformed *Nayeeka*.

In the Bangladesh television, maturity in the central women lead had not been uncommon in the past. In the recent times though, it is becoming rare. Like the fashion world of the west the women roles in the privately produced TV dramas have only the very young in the central lead and the story is of a courtship prior to marriage. This has also been the norm of cinema. The very narrow span of life and situation, covered of the women excludes and obliterates all other experiences in her life. In the process it re-inforces the stereotyped *Nayeeka* situation once again.

The activity too of the woman "lead" negatively contributes in the construction of her image. Apart from the dialogues it is important to evaluate "business" given to the women in the role she plays. More often she is before the mirror combing her hair or doing the bed. One of our most famous playwright's female leads are criticized for persistently making and serving tea to the family. Thus, in the middle class household, it is most common activity of the woman to keep the rest of the family in constant supply of tea, however it is also a common phenomenon that she studies, reads the newspaper or works on the computer. However these business are but very rarely depicted in the women roles on TV. To be informed, makes the position of a person strong. Our new woman of the 'media' could be shown as informed and activities could well of reading a book than stirring the tea.

The plays of Bangladesh television are also stuck in the groove of the middle class since the middle class sentiments are very marketable for the masses, or so it is assumed. The middle position of this class is easier to treat and gives scope for romanticism using the middle class sentiment. The lower income group is fleetingly touched upon when the support class of servants have to be depicted. To depict the villainy, or the social wrongs, the upper income people are depicted in the stereotyped roles as "bad people". The middle class values puts a limit to the "woman lead" which may be overcome by her if she can take a bold step beyond this boundary adding yet another dimension to the new *Nayeeka.* For example the virtual absence of say, a garment worker in a central position is an under representation of this huge workforce, and it is only indicative of the narrowness of the media's range of vision. Thus the heroine is usually a student who belongs to a middle income household whose future, other than being the ideal match to her partner, is never a concern for the playwright. That the women are coming into the workforce and the ups & downs of her career, and threats thereof can be of equal interest as her affairs to the audience, seems beyond the conception of most playwrights.

Given that the world of "showbiz" supported by the "commerce" will continue to place women in the centre and under the male gaze, it is well that the new *Nayeeka* is shaped in the place of the stereotyped *Nayeeka*, men think are ideal and continue to construct in their blissful ignorance.

IMAGES OF WOMEN IN HINDI CINEMA: POST 1950S

Shabana Azmi

I begin with a quote from noted filmcritic Aruna Vasudev. "It is no coincidence that the first Indian film was a mythological. The moral education of all but the thinnest layer of affluent, westernised looking Indians is derived from the epics. These stories, despite liberal doses of miracles and fantasy, are no fairy tales easily told and forgotten. They still have a living reality and a dominant say in the conduct of daily life today".

Unfortunately for the women of India, the example of Sita as the perfect wife acquiescing unquestioningly to her husband's rejection of her has been held up as the ideal for any women to follow. Taken in conjunction with Manu — the law giver, the average women in India has had no opportunities to become anything more than the role to which she has been restricted as daughter, wife and mother. In chapter 9 verse 3 of the *Manu Smriti* — Manu is quoted as saying "In childhood a female must be subject to her father, in youth to her husband, when her lord is dead to her sons. A woman does not deserve freedom. She must not seek to separate herself from her father, husband, sons. She must always be cheerful, clear in the management of her household affairs, careful in cleaning her utensils, economical in expenditure. Him, to whom her father may give her, or her brother with the father's permission, she shall obey as long as he lives and when he is dead, she must not insult his memory". With these few lines women were condemned for 2,000 years to life of eternal subjection. Tradition required it, today the cinema enthusiastically upholds it. In film after we see these values re-iterated, underlined and reinforced.

To the weight of this tradition is added a middle class morality which makes a sharp distinction between women as wife and mother, and women as mistress and lover. Subscribing to the predominantly orthodox views of the large majority of audiences rather than acknowledge the reality of women's growing influence and contribution to society, film makers generally prefer perceptions of the status of women which perpetuate male domination in society. As such, these portrayals reflect the society not so much as it is evolving as the way they may wish it to remain.

Popular cinema creates instant mythologies for uncritical consumption and not histories of credible people. The heroine is cast in two moulds:

a. The all forgiving, self-sacrificing wife;
b. The virtuous upholder of morality, the nurturing mother;
c. The 'other' women-vamp, titillating 'siren';
d. Courtesan with a heart of gold.

Hindi Cinema in the 1980s and 1990s has not really progressed beyond these cardboard stereotypes. Like noted film critic Maithili Rao says, "The true archetypes of popular cinema are only two. First is the *Mother India's* matriarch who is the upholder of *dharma* and the true emotional centre of the hero's life. The second is *Pakeezah*, the romanticised apostrophe to women as the pathetic impossible innocent 'other' to be rescued from the penumbra of social opprobrium. Every *Tawaif* and her cousin is descended from *Pakeezah* and is a man's reflection of pale, derived poetic pathos and every mother sternly casting out her son, is *Mother India's* daughter".

Radha, as portrayed by Nargis in *Mother India* is a truly iconic archetype in the sense that she is simple, strong and stern without the complexity that assails most modern individuals. *Mother India's* appeal is not only emotional and dramatic as the nurturing mother who stoically faces every adversity heaped on her. From tender bride to respected matriarch, her whole identity and purpose in life is nurturing her children. She is conceived as the enforcer of *Dharma*. The two sons are obviously derived from the two mythical heroes — Rama and Krishna. The younger Birju is the dark prankster with a penchant for dispensing rough and ready justice. And it is the passionate Birju that the mother loves most. But this conflict between duty and love is not allowed to cloud her judgment or impede the inevitability of her action. Mother India's path is sternly and immutably fixed.

Over the years it was easy to make this potent image with all its uncomplicated simplicity and apply it to an urban, contemporary setting as in *Diwar*, *Agneepath* and *Khalnayak*. The mother figure has a prominent place in the cast of characters of most Hindi films, none of which ever speak of a relationship between mother and daughter. Even with the sons, it is not so much a relationship that is explored or portrayed as the deification of the mother. Self-sacrificing, maligned and victimised by fate or the husband, she is shown as indestructible when it comes to protecting her sons. Since the heroine is strait-jacketed into a chaste wife whose suffering can only make her more virtuous, she can never assert her sexuality. No real relationship can develop with a wife who is a potential mother/goddess and must be pure and sexless creature. With whom, then can a man have a satisfying relationship, physical and emotional? The courtesan has been a significant figure in classical Indian literature and until the 1970's, a staple diet of the Hindi films. Since she is forever excluded from the pale of domesticity, she can answer his physical needs, later to his fantasies (unlike the wife whose purpose is to procreate). Of course he may not fall in love with her, but inevitably her heart is lost to him. She provides solace, a haven when he recovers from his sorrows — he goes away or she conveniently swallows a diamond and dies.

The cultivated *Tawaif* is not merely a pathetic victim of male lust. Around her, is a cluster of myths and romantic yearning, of neatly labelling women as the exciting 'other' and the wife as boring in her virtue. She is the melancholic music of romantic poetry, the graceful arbiter of courtly manners, the siren who lures with song and dance. She was different from the vamp of Indian cinema. The vamp from Hindi cinema, a popular figure from 1950's onwards becomes a staple diet in the film of the 1960s and early 1970s. The vamp was seen as an outsider, a home breaker who could display wanton sexuality on the screen. This display of sexuality was restricted to certain spaces of the Hindi screen, for example, the night clubs, the bar, the casino etc. These were moral spaces associated with the West, which through our own history of colonialism, were seen as evil. The association of sexuality with the West had the effect of denying Indian women their own sexuality. The vamp was thus contrasted with the heroine of Hindi cinema, a woman who was virtuous, chaste, pure and spiritual. Helen played an extremely important role in the films of the 1960s as she was able to carry the Western image very easily.

In the cinema of the 90s, we see that vamp, who was crucial to the narrative of earlier cinema, has almost disappeared from the screen. This exit has been significant to the narrative of earlier cinema, has almost disappeared from the screen. This exit has been significant and is being seen with both fear and concern since the heroine of the 90s also carried within her the image of the vamp. New levels of permissiveness have obliterated the strictly enforced divide between the heroine and the vamp. The rigid dress code has disappeared. Today's heroine dances with the seductive abandon of a *houri* as the camera routinely zooms in on one body part or the other. Her titillating purpose done, she usually dons a demure sari towards the end as she attains the "highly desirable" wife status.

The conflation of the heroine and the vamp of yesteryears into a single image of the heroine is disturbing many because the question of sexuality which was essentially seen as wantonness associated with the west and thus outside of Indian culture, is no longer being seen as something to be rejected. The heroine of today seems to be questioning the image of fixing the heroine into a slot where any display of desire was seen as negative and unlike the values of Indian women (with exceptions like *Sahib Bibi aur Ghulam* — Meena Kumari asserts her sexuality and demands that her husband stay back with her and takes to alcohol... ultimately dies tragically).

While the new image questions the moral codes that operated on the heroine of yesteryears, it would be wrong to celebrate this change uncritically. The business of films is to create the more potent its mythical seemingly indestructible life. The film image ostensibly celebrates the heroine's eroticism, while reducing her to a passive sex object. Much as one might wish to argue that Karishma Kapoor seems to be an active participant rather than a passive recipient of Govinda's lust — the fact cannot be denied that she is being subjected to the male gaze. The film *Choli Ke Peechey*, while ostensibly celebrating a women's early sexuality is picturised in a way — where her body is fragmented into heaving bosom, swinging hip, bare midriff — commodifies her into an object for the overwhelming male gaze and robs her of all autonomy over her body.

The change that is taking place in the women of the Hindi cinema is a confused one — whereas the earlier films like *Main Chup Rahungi* (I will remain silent) being considered a virtue in itself, are giving way to a different female protagonist — the avenging angel *Zahhmee Aurat, Sherni, Insaf Ki Devi,* etc., inevitably show a female vigilante sworn to vengeance after the trauma of rape. Do these films offer any insights into the complexities of what it means to be a women.

It is only cosmetic change. First we had Rambos, now we have Rambolinas — men in drag wearing figure — hugging leather jeans, with a gun in one hand, purely imitating the cardboard one dimensional hero!

It was left to the parallel cinema to give women their due. The attempt of the *new wave* cinema was to situate women in real life conditions as social beings and not as either objects of display or servile, static creatures. The agenda of the *new wave* was directed against the main stream and thus a spate of films emerged with strong women character. Films like *Ankur, Bhoomika, Nishant, Manthan,* etc., become well known for their strong women characters. While the women of these films were no doubt strong, they were limited in their agenda by the politics of realism that was a major influence on the *new wave* cinema. In attempting reality on the screen, the films makers were always restricted by the oppressive conditions that prevented women from attaining any kind of freedom in society. The *new wave* was, thus, marked by a series of compromises that the women always made and was justified in the name of "reality" (e.g., *Manthan, Bhoomika*). The women thus never ceased to be victims of society in the New wave barring exceptions like *Mirch Masala*, sections of *Mandi,* etc. In urban situations, the dominant narrative became an exploration of the women's self rather than situating women in their social context — this turning the quest for woman's freedom into a struggle within the private sphere alone. The woman, having an affair with a man other than her husband, being seen as an ultimate act of feminist revolt e.g., *Ek Pal, Paroma, Dristi,* etc.

It is however, becoming amply evident that society and cinema can no longer close their eyes to the changing Indian women. Self assured confined women are starting to back out of the economic dependence that had for so long held them in thrall. In a society in transition, the rigidity of part norms cannot be maintained.

But who is this new woman? How much liberty can she be "granted" without threatening the very basis of a patriarchal order. What aspect of her personality should be highlighted? Even if a daring premise is taken, isn't it safer to stay with a resolution that is conformist?

A hero is the personification of contemporary morality and aspirations till such time as society can work out what this new women is all about. The transformation of stereotypes with icons will continue to be confused.

In a situation where stereotypes play such an important role in defining the way we make sense of the world, it is clear that a pure space outside the stereotype is difficult to imagine. Thus the quest for women's representation on the screen should move beyond just a critique of stereotyping of a more complex dialogue and debate about the plurality of women's imagery — a plurality that needs to recognise that women's representation cannot be seen as only a 'positive' or negative image but as an arena of contesting voices and faces. It is finally upto us to recover the resistant voice/moments within this area.

Acknowledgments Aruna Vasudev — *The Women Vamp or Victim*. Maithili Rao — *To be a Women*. *Shikha Thingan vs Ranjam Mazumdar*.

WOMEN IN INDIAN DANCE

Sonal Mansingh

The tradition of performing arts in India has been dominated by women. As singers, dancers and actresses, women lent grace, beauty and rainbow dimensions to art and culture. Festivals, marriage, celebrations of every kind, varied events of everyday life were never complete without the presentations of song and dance usually performed by women. More specifically Dance or *Nritya* which was an amalgam of music, poetic texts of great myths, legends and philosophical concepts sat on the apex of cultural values that informed and shaped successive civilisations across the Indian sub-continent.

The oldest known Indian text on theatre, the *Bharata Natya Shastra* speaks of dance as a social grace of infinite value for the performer and viewer alike. Well-trained women danced for an assembly of connoisseurs called *RASIKA-SABHA*. Their critical appreciation was sought more than favours from a king. This was the earliest known place of performance of dance. Then came the chieftains and kings who were entertained by court-dancers. A king being the mortal representative of God on earth, in turn offered dancers, dedicating them to the presiding deity of the temple. Thus, the three levels in later times came to be known as *Samauya-Dasi, Raja-Dasi and Deva-dasi.* They influenced the thinking, attitudes and mores of their times more than can be imagined today.

Whereas no auspicious or festive occasion was deemed complete without a proper performance of dance by women, with the changing social patterns and patriarchichal trends they began to be considered lowly or as fallen women. Dance itself being an art-form at once to physical and vivid when performed by comely young women had the undeniable power of capturing heads and hearts of Gods and men alike. The supple and smooth limbs wore magic tapestry of gestures and postures. That beckoned, cajoled or spurned the viewer's attention. But then even Shiva The Great God has the epithet Nataraja-King of Dancers and Krishna is called *Nata-Nagara* the Dancing Dandy. All the Gods and Goddesses, sages and seers, Emperors and noblemen had to gain proficiency in the twin arts of Dance and Music. For it gave poise, power, grace, harmonious thoughts, balanced posture and a rootedness in themselves which were not to be got from any other activity. Indeed, dance and music came to be considered as the shortest path to *Enlightenment.*

Earliest known model of a dancer is supposedly from excavations at *Mohen-jo-Dairo*, about 6000 years ago, of a bronze figurine of a saucy young woman with high breasts, right arms akimbo on the hip and with one knee flexed in a posture known is *A-bhanga*. The second century B.C. rock-cut sculpture of a court-scene of *King Kharavela* of Orissa shows two buxom dancers flanked by musicians playing on percussion and wing instruments. Innumerable depictions in sculpture, frescoes, textiles, and old manuscripts show similar scenes of abandon in dance and music. Women dominate these scenes as do their beauty and shapely bodies. By virtue of their naturally voluptuous physical endowments, female dancers at once became the most coveted, honoured yet feared creatures. Through dance they could wield power over natural phenomena, flora, fauna and humans. They could invoke the blessings and grace (*Kripa*) of Gods and add fertility to soil. They were always the honoured citizens of the Kingdom, rewarded and awarded best tracts of agricultural land, palatial mansions, jewellery and fine silks and a retinue of servants.

Increasing aggressions from alien tribes who brought alien set of values and a fractured vision of life found the sensuousness and beauty of the dances in India strangely overpowering and contrary to their own religious and 'moral' beliefs. Therefore the dance, dancers, musicians and *Gurus*—all had to be discouraged and the performers scattered off to live anonymously in unknown villages. The suppression of dance and its philosophy in India is a depressing chapter of Indian history. Yet, with the advent of nationalist fervour preceding independence, many men and women took up re-establishment of dance-traditions as their cause. Famous among them include *Smt. Rukmini Devi Arundala* who set up *Kalakshetra, Smt. Menaka* who revived *Kathak* dance, poet *Rabindranath Tagore* who pioneered a new style of dancing now known as Tagore School of dance greatly influenced by *Manipuri* style.

Today, learning to dance is considered a major accomplishment for young girls and women and dancing as a profession/vocation is back in vogue albeit to audiences who may be a mixed bag of aficionados, connoisseurs, curious onlookers, tourists, diplomats and politicians.

Recurrent themes in Indian dance-texts and poetry paint the image of woman in prismatic images as:

DEVI (shining effulgent Being)
SATI
KANYA
KUMARI

At other levels she is the *NAYIKA*, the leader, the inspirer, a reward at the end of a long emotional journey. She is the creatrix and destroyer—giver and nourisher who reserves the right to punish as Mother. She is the focal point of creation and has the power to hold household, family, society and civilisations together. Indian dance has celebrated the multi-faceted, multi-layered, multi-dimensional persona of woman with depiction of arch-type characters like *Durga, Radha, Draupadi, Sita, Ahalya, Meera, Mahadenakka, Muktabai, Rani Jhansi, Kasturba Gandhi* and thousands of others. Myth and history merge in India as nowhere else in the world. Because history speaks only of the past, whereas myth speaks at once of the past, present and future.

My own dance understanding has veered more and more towards women-oriented themes which become metaphors for our times. In an era of social and political insecurity where women attain to high positions, the majority remain at levels of suffering, unspeakable cruelty, torture — both physical and mental and humiliations meted out by society in the name of religion, ethics, morality or convenience. Traditions are deliberately misinterpreted, facts twisted and natural order of things reversed. I personally agree with many that much-maligned author of *Manu-Smriti* who declared *Yatra Naryastu Pujyante Ramante Tara Devala.* Divine grace descends only where women as venerated, honoured and esteemed.

The solo-dance-theatre *DRAUPADI* is one such example of a dancer's attempt to address the age-old problems confronting women and to point at relevant issues to checkout if things have changed at all.

Mayaa hi sarvam jetavyam
Aham na jeyo kenachit

(Everything is to be conquered by me, I by nobody and nothing)

The Shared Imagination and Cooperation in South Asia: Nepalese Perspective

Durga Prasad Bhandari

It is bold on the part of the Centre for Policy Dialogue to have selected a new theme for the 1995/96 Dialogue. Exploring the shared values captured in the creative imagination of South Asia is not so manageable an enterprise as I thought it to be. There is such a commonality of vision and voice in the South Asian creative imagination, that it is very hard to tell the Bangladeshi imagination from the Indian imagination, Indian from the Nepali and vice versa. Yet it is worthwhile to find out the native uniqueness and peculiarity if there is any. What overwhelms one at the very thought of such endeavour is to embark on the adventure of going through the familiar and unfamiliar creative genres. Human rights and social justice, position of women and secularism, communalism and sectarianism are in their character very much common to all the SAARC countries. Nevertheless it is stimulating to take a look at the difference of perception.

Nepal is a country with a political identity and historical consciousness like all the SAARC countries and with comparatively greater and longer isolation like a few of its members. The imaginative and the intellectual, the intuitive and the logical faculty of any country or society is determined by the course of its cultural history right up to the present moment. The "challenge and response" theory of Arnold Toyanbee, a great thinker and historian of this century is worth recalling while contemplating about the texture and quality of a culture. If the response matches the challenge a great culture can be born, if the matching is unequal then it tends to slide towards masculine or feminine way, extrovert or introvert. It seems to me that all the SAARC countries are introvert societies — some are more introvert than others. We can classify the societies as introvert and extrovert as we classify the individuals. SAARC is a conglomerate of introvert societies barring the few episodes of racial invasion and assertiveness in the past. But they are all unitedly and individually trying to be more outward looking, more assertive than they were half a century ago. They seem to be determined to face up to the situation that their own history has presented to them. They have many things in common — common heritage, common aspirations for the future, common ambitions to work for a fellowship of the free nations of the world. We, all the dialogue-makers at the Dhaka meet will attempt to explore how our creative artists have looked into the position of women, the question of secularism and the question of human rights and social justice in our individual society. And the creative imagination of India, Pakistan, Bangladesh and Nepal is essentially lyrical. A lyrical imagination is pulled more powerfully by the past than by the future. Even in our most prosaic moments we tend to be lyrical. By lyrical I mean the South Asian mind-set is sentimental and nostalgic; it talks more often than not of the golden past that has left us and of the golden future that is yet to come. When we talk more of the present reality we do not become interesting to ourselves. Yet we are compelled to talk because we have to live in the present.

Nepal has enough reason to be proud of having produced some creative artists in the twentieth century who can be ranked with the important artists of other South Asian Countries and beyond. They have seen the position of women, the human rights and social justice, communalism, secularism and sectarianism with the vision of creative mind, not with the loud perspective of the politician, social reformer and a policy maker. What is true about one genuine artist is usually true about the other artist. I cannot not think any literary artist, any painter or sculptor can be ostensible and declarative in his objective. He is for the most part subtle and impressive in his creations. Any creations with a manifesto to redress the social ills has the inherent danger of falling into a vulgar sloganeering and pamphleteering which is unfortunately called by a certain set of people as the real aim of art. The artists I have in mind are the artists who are free from the prejudice of any reformist and didactic zeal. At the moment I am inspired to recall — rightly or wrongly — Rabindranath Tagore, Laxmi Prasad Devkota, Saadat Hasan Manto, Kazi Nazrul Islam. Manto and Islam, in spite of their obsession with social realism, did transcend it in some of their great writings. In fact a great artist is one whose creation combines both time and timelessness. I have in my mind great painters and sculptors, great producers and directors of theatrical art, great classical and folk artists, with my limited understanding of the classical art in its different expressions. My attempt to deal with the art forms other than literature might sound gratuitous, irrelevant and superficial. I will try to discover how all the three issues are reflected in the best known dramatic poem of Mahakavi Laxmi Prasad Devkota and will also take a passing look at some of the representative Nepali literary artists. Devkota's magnum opus is *Munamadan*, the master narrative for my purpose at the moment.

Munamadan is thoroughly rooted in Nepali soil; the theme, the rhythm the metre, the conception and execution, everything about the poem is unaffectedly Nepali, the first and last of Devkota's great poems without the impress of any external influence. Most of his works bear out the direct or subtle influence of the classical Sanskrit Poetry and the English romantic poetry. *Munamadan* in its idiom, energy, naturalness and flowing cadence stands out unique in Nepali literature, perhaps in South Asian literature.

The sublime emotion is expressed with meticulous artistic maturity in the speech of the most common man. *Munamadan* is a folk tale refined into a beautiful lyrical poem of love, separation and death. It is presented in different forms — ballet, dance drama, painting and special poetic recitation since it appeared in print in 1935. And the poem which is very small in size — forty pages — has made immense impact upon Nepali literature and upon the Nepali psyche. In those days these issues of human rights, of women, of communalism and secularism did not bother the Asian mind much with a few individual exceptions. It was inconceivable even to imagine that Nepali artists under the family autocracy could overtly or covertly plead for the human rights, women's rights and secularism. In fact the formal recognition of human rights came much later even in the west. Devkota was a rebel as all great artists are rebels in some sense, but he was a rebel not at the cost of art. He was not happy with the state of things in his country; at the same time he could not demonstrate his unhappiness through his writings in a manner detectable by the autocratic rulers and their minions. He was at his subtlest in all those poems which have the veiled message for his own time and beyond his time.

Muna is the wife, Madan the husband who have still retained the fervor and heat of lovers who can sacrifice and surrender whatever they have on earth and heaven for each other. Madan, a high caste Kshetri decides to go to Bhote, Tibet, to make a living. Muna stays back at home to attend to his old ailing mother, but her mind is occupied with the thought of Madan and gets nearly wild in her imaginings. Madan is suddenly taken ill and is looked after by the alien Bhote, the lowborn tribal of high Tibet. The human quality of the poor Bhote touched Madan's heart. In return Madan touches her feet trying to convince him with these words.

> A son of high Kshetri touches these
> feet with love unbounded
> Any man is great not because of his cast
> but because of his heart.

The strong caste barrier and communal division widely prevalent in those days is ridiculed by Devkota in *Munamadan* and other works.

Madan makes a significant comment on the state or position of women not in any particular society but in the whole scheme of creation. Madan tells Muna: "Woman is holding the whole responsibility of creating the present and future and she has been giving delight and fragrance to human existence since time immemorial." Devkota could not be so crude to say that 'yet women are being discriminated against by every society'. Devkota in *Munamadan, Shakuntala* and other poems and dramas is always upholding the case of women and the downtrodden with his characteristic artistic delicacy. By any definition Devkota is a humanist who (if he were alive today) would have been vigorously defending the issue of human rights, including the rights of women, and would have been sincerely and powerfully sending the message to his audience that religious, communal, and ethnic harmony is essential for the healthy growth of any society. He has questioned the rationale of orthodoxy and obscurantism in some of his poems unafraid of the rulers' whip.

Mahakavi Devkota is a poet of highest creative imagination in Nepali Literature. In his creative days under the dictatorial regime panegyric writing was more or less customary for all kinds of writers — creative or non-creative. Devkota deliberately refrained from dedicating poems to the rulers and praising their repressive rule. He was completely given to his muse to the end of his life. His casual eccentricity and indifference to the practical aspect of life is a mark of a man who is creatively and spiritually above the common run of men. This is to say that he not only created great poetry, he also lived it and lived it in a very uncongenial age. Some of his shorter poems along with *Munamadan* and *Shakuntala* will live for all times. If any one ever tries to discover a message in his poetry he will find that Devkota is above every thing else a humanist who happened to be born about a hundred years before his time. Without letting him know most of the poets of modern Nepali literature have taken him to their heart as their guiding spirit. Impalpably *Munamadan* has made a seminal impact upon the Nepalese psyche.

Next to Devkota, because of my limited knowledge of Nepali literature, I feel compelled to recall B.P. Koirala for his obvious relevance for the given issues we are going to discuss in the dialogue. He has earned a considerable reputation as a short story writer and as a novelist who has invariably taken human society and human mind for his theme. Curiously enough politics which has been his lifelong vocation has never for a moment restrained his literary output. His creative writing are neatly detached from his political ideology. *Sumnima* is the title of his most important novel he wrote in prison (1970), (almost all his novels were written in prison). He has here given a highly balanced and penetrating insight into the question of ethnicity and communalism in Nepal.

Som Dutta, a Brahmin who takes a vow to lead a life of celibacy and austerity as is prescribed by the Shastras and his immediate ancestors, falls in love with Sumnima, a girl from the putative lowborn Kirati community who is comparatively free in matter of sexual and social behaviour. Som Dutta does everything externally impressive towards the fulfilment of ascetic destiny. But he cannot go very long with the ascetic discipline. He falls, falls into the embrace of Sumnima and he finds his fulfilment instead. He is traditionally married to Puloma, a woman of his caste who is also internally drawn to another man. Sumnima is much more drawn to Som Dutta. The pairs are not comfortable with the conventional roles they are supposed to play. The women break the age old social respectability and look for greater freedom. The mutual gravitation of Sumnima and Som Dutta is an embodiment of communal harmony and of longing for psychological and social freedom. B.P., by making the high caste Puloma attach to the low caste man is sending an obvious message to his audience that the concept of high and low only in terms of caste and community is irrational and stupid. The theme of ethnicity is deftly dramatized in this novel. The kind of social scenario and ethnic problem reflected in the novel is a characteristic South Asian reality. The women of B.P. Koirala are comparatively more unorthodox in temperament and social behaviour than the women of other Nepali writers. There are, of course, a few tradition-bound women who stand as a contrast to the tradition-questioning women. Koirala's men do not look so important as his women. His stories and novels together fascinate his readers for three reasons: his deep psychological insight, his insinuation of social, psychological and moral message, artistic balance, and the mild thrust upon the liberation of human from the irrelevant dogmas, rituals, and superstition. Above all Koirala is a writer for harmony — communal, social psychological, biological and religious. Yet this great politician never talks of politics in his creative writings. Woman is at the centre of his works.

Gopal Prasad Rimal, a playwright and a poet makes poverty, social, injustice and the liberation of women the leitmotif of his writings. Both in thought and technique, he breaks the convention of moving around only the old religious and social stereotype. In his play *Masan* he frees the principal woman from the tyranny of her husband and the repressive domestic atmosphere in the same way as Ibsen does free Nora in Doll's House. *Masan* was written about fifty years ago.

Govinda Bahadur Gothale wrote *Pallo Gharko Jhyal* (the window of the other house). The window is a symbol looking out for a woman who has been confined in the room for centuries. She leaves home to start a new life with the man she sees outside that window. A symbolic representation of woman's desire to be free and become herself is the burden of the novel. Similarly the play *Bhoosko Ago* (fire in the husk) dramatizes the feelings and problems of women.

Parijat, a powerful woman novelist in her most popular novel *Shirisko Phool* (1965) introduced the theme of woman's predicament and her position in a male dominated society. She shows men getting frightened by the presence of free spirited women, on matter how physically frail and delicate they are. Parijat's women are independent or on the road to independence; they are becoming more and more resolute not to be men's shadows.

Bhoopi Sherchan, a popular modern poet is satirical and epigrammatic in these lines which are among the most quoted from the anthology of his poems:

> When I constantly see young Sitas
> In the streets, the alleys, the markets,
> In my country and in foreign lands,
> Stripped bare like eucalyptus trees,
> When I see countless Bhimsen Thapas,
> Standing still and silent, ...
> I really feel like mocking my blood.

Bhoopi here laments the degeneration of the ideal for which we have been living and dying for ages. The old values are juxtaposed with modern reality.

More recent poets than Bhoopi in Nepali literature also have taken society, politics and the eternal thirst for love as the staple of their poetry. In the 1990 movement for democracy, they got particularly articulate. They got the occasion and excuse to express themselves uninhibited. During the Panchayat rule the literary artists and others — quite a number of them — were excited at times to give articulation to their feelings at a considerable risk. The artistic minds generally revolt against repression and injustice. Most of them talk and assert for human rights denied under a ruthless dispensation. I believe circumstances, both political and social, are very common to the SAARC countries, also the desire to improve or tolerate them in the artists is very common.

Drama and theatre has undergone changes in the last fifteen years. The street theatre is a new phenomenon in the subcontinent. The emergence of *Sarvanaam*, a street theatre group in 1981 is an important event. A perceptive critic in Nepali literature, Abhi Subedi says, "The Sarvanaam Street Theatre started at a time when it was not possible to dramatize even within the four walls, the desire for free expression. What could not be said within the four walls was, however said openly by the Sarvanaam in the Street." And the Sarvanaam said on most of the occasions in favor of human rights, social justice, in favour of the improvement in the condition of women, and in favour of ethnic integration, harmony, and ethnic participation in the affairs of the country. They said it with a great deal of seriousness and intensity. Very recently, some five years ago, well known groups from most countries of South Asia staged their performance in Kathmandu. It was an extraordinary experience. The drama showed that the problems and aspirations of the region are similar. Issues like human rights, women's position, poverty, exploitation, democracy were the principal themes. Ashesh Malla, the dramatist, was the main organizer. Badal Sarcar, generally called the father of street theatre in India was fully participating and sharing experiences. If Safdar Hashmi were alive he would also have come to take part in the Kathmandu dramatic festival. All important participants talked nostalgically of him.

The television serials to some extent, the non commercial cinemas to some extent, the commercials to some extent reflect the suffering of women, and new awakening in them to revolt against their unjust domination by men and society. Some movies like *Ujeli* and *Chelibeti* demonstrate the suffering of women who cannot complain, who cannot articulate what they feel; they accept suffering as an inevitable part of their destiny. But the response in the sensitive audience is the sense of disgust and protest. Nepal TV is, I hear, planning to make more films on communal harmony, on the evils of poverty, illiteracy; on social justice and on women and their right to be equal with men. The serials and cinema's made on these issues so far are too small a number to be satisfied with. Nepal Radio is doing fairly a good job on this score.

Contemporary Nepali paintings reflect not always but sometimes in the artists' compassionate moments the issues of human rights, women's condition, communal discord and communal concord with considerable poignance and sharpness. In the manner of modern poetry paintings too embody the themes of freedom. Many modern paintings done under the title of "Democracy" present a new scenario. The brush strokes, the prominents use of primary colours and the mobility of images in the paintings of Lainsingh Bangdel, Kiran Manandhar and other young artists, the vision of apocalypse in the *Kalkiavatar* series of Shashi Shah dramatise in the visual form the thirst for freedom and change.

Women artists also are coming up with amazing brilliance. Ragini Upadhyaya's recent paintings present very successfully the themes of women, their position in the traditional society. She shows them by the use of familiar themes, archetypes and the use of familiar colour. "Ragini's political paintings do not project the grim and violent post modernist images of the political myth of the recent times" says Abhi Subedi. Shashikala Tiwari links women and environment, and the predicament of women. There is profusion of blue and green in her art.

There has been occasional exchange and interaction among the creative minds of South Asia. Almost every year painting exhibition of Nepali paintings is organized in Dhaka. Some time ago Nepali and Bangladeshi artists jointly exhibited their works in Kathmandu.

Writers of the region, officially or privately, visit each other's countries. Whenever there is political change in the subcontinent the writers want to come closer and share each others hearts and minds. The sharing may prompt them to work in unison. Further sharing might be stimulated by the fifth Dhaka Dialogue. I believe it holds a great promise. The awareness of making a dialogue about the creative imagination of five countries is in itself a remarkable step towards moving closer to the real understanding of each others' problems. In reality the outer manifestation in any form — war, peace, human rights, social justice, woman's agony, communal harmony or conflict, religious or political dogmatism, fundamentalism — is an indicator of what we have been inwardly feeling and thinking and how we have been expressing ourselves through the medium of arts for many generations. South Asia or for that matter any part of the world is what it is on the strength of it's inner growth of inward journey in the creative imagination. Lord Buddha is creative in the ultimate, supreme sense, Shakespeare is creative in the sense we usually understand creativity and creative imagination. There is, I repeat, an overwhelming commonality of creative imagination in South Asia, because there is some commonality of sources and roots that has been shaping the South Asian mind for many centuries. The tangible is drawing upon the intangible, upon the subterranean. Besides, the geography and history of the region has been passing through more or less the similar vicissitude. We have been holding dialogue with each other for centuries, but the dialogue of this time is going to be of unique character. Certainly this will "break a new ground."

An academic commonplace to-day is that the major factor determining social peace and prosperity is culture — a sense of common identity, tradition and value. This South Asian dialogue is presumably a search in that direction. Culture is created by the artists, seers and thinkers. The folk culture also has its roots and branches in the artistic thinking and behavior of any society, tribal or sophisticated. Each of these five countries has its own cultural identity. If all countries merge together they create a greater whole and greater responsibility to keep individual identity on the one hand and to develop a resilience and openness for the regional, subcontinental, continental and intercontinental communion and oneness on the other which should be the mark of a great cultural undertaking. This is essential to liberate ourselves from the religious bigotry and pettiness, from nationalist egotism and from much of the hypocrisy of the present day world whose staple of dialogue and conversation is politics and economics more than anything else. The fifth South Asia Dialogue will hopefully prove that talking of culture which encompasses among other things literatures, painting, theatre, cinema, folklore can be more fascinating and equally profitable.

To give a picture of the regional creative imagination even on these much talked about issues is nearly impossible within the limited space of time and of the paper; to give a cogent picture of what the creative artists of my country have imagined, referred to, alluded or directly dealt with is very difficult. Is has become very difficult for me. And despite my dissatisfaction with myself I am obliged to take it as a pious task to put before this distinguished gathering whatever I have discovered with my desultory effort. The great or not so great artists in South Asia — most of them — have displayed their sense of revolt against tyranny, injustice, sluggishness, fundamentalism, dogmatism, excessive nationalism, repression of men and women and any kind of superstition. Laxmi Prasad Devkota, completely uncorrupted by any obvious political opinion or ideology, or any obvious enthusiasm for the improvement of his society has very artistically — if we want to find — expressed about the position of woman and what it ought to be, about the dignity of man and woman in an undignified world, about the oneness and harmony of all human communities and castes, about the god who dwells in every body's hearts irrespective of colour, caste, birth and gender. In his short poem *Temple* and *To a Beautiful Prostitute*, he is an uncompromising humanist, unparalleled in Nepal literature.

I know next to nothing about the most renowned Bengali poet Kazi Nazrul Islam. However, on the basis of what I read long ago of Islam I venture to say that he was an iconoclast and a humanist of great understanding. His *Rebel* is a work which comprehends all the issues of our Dialogue and at the same time transcends them. He was a great artist and a great egalitarian. I know very little of Pakistani literature. And I do not know where to put Galib and Meer and other pre-independence writers: in India or in Pakistan. Iqbal was Pakistani by choice and by temperament. I love Galib, Meer, Faiz and Ahmad Faraz. Iqbal was a great poet but not as equally lovable for the secular minded readers. His lines such as *Allahake sheronko aati nahin rubahi*[8] smacks of something less than the humanistic abandon and poetic amplitude of Galib, Meer, Faiz Ahamad Faiz and Ahmad Faraz. Saadat Hassan Manto, a remarkable story writer writes about the poor, the down-trodden and the lowliest in the society with an extraordinary boldness of treatment. Manto the story teller in the recent past and Faraz the poet in contemporary Pakistan have carried the fire of revolt against injustice and brutality in the society. Manto for example writes in his story *Thanda Gost.* "A prostitute is a helpless and friendless woman. Every day hundreds of men come to her carrying a single desire. But even in the midst of those who desire her she is alone." Devkota's prostitute is also apparently a victim of social injustice, but spiritually she is higher than the so-called high caste women. Manto presents his helplessness as it is, Devkota idealises it. Both are compassionate and wish her to come out of the mire. Devkota is oblique in castigating the society, Manto is straight.

Whatever the similarly and difference in the artistic expression of the subcontinent the creative imagination on the whole is multidimensional. It seems moving from the "foul rag — and bone shop of the heart" to the splendid heights of metaphysics and spiritualism. The most known and the best example of multidimensional creative imagination is Rabindranath Tagore who is simultaneously moved by the smell of the earth and the fragrance of heaven. Here he sings of the mystic ecstasy, there he shudders at the colossal poverty, widespread social injustice and expanding religious and communal insularity in the Indian society. His heart is filled with "awe and wonder" at the celestial glory above and "the uncontrollable mystery of the bestial floor" below. Tagore prays to the Almighty to free his countrymen from all kinds of pettiness, injustice, inhumanity, repression and narrow mindedness, and prays that India be a land "where the heart is without fear and the head is held high, *chitta jetha bhaya shunya, uccha jetha shir.*"

---

[8] The lions of God know no cowardice.

IMAGES OF THE FEMALE IN SRI LANKAN ART

Sirima Kiribamune

In the words of the Convenors of the South Asia dialogue what is attempted at this meeting is exploring "the shared perceptions of our artists in the way they reflect certain values and attitudes of fundamental concern to our societies". My presentation is related to only a small part of this vast exploratory field and has to do with looking at how pre-modern Sri Lankan creative artists have addressed the issue of the position of women in society. The values and attitudes reflected in these creations need to be placed in the wider context of South Asia so that the present discussions can lead to a combined exploration of the roles and status of women in our societies.

A point that I need to draw attention to at the very outset of this exercise is that the "shared perceptions of our artists" in the present study are almost exclusively male perceptions. So what we are basically looking at are perceptions of male sculptors and painters regarding the social roles and position of women. The missing element in this is women's own perceptions of their roles and status in society. The almost total absence of known sculptors and painters among women is not a particularly Sri Lankan phenomenon and neither is it an Asian occurrence. The question as to why this is so would go beyond the parameters of a South Asian dialogue. It would suffice to say that one has to constantly keep in mind that the female in art is mostly a male preoccupation. Let me, however, hasten to add that artists, male or female, are not immune to their environment. The attitudes and pressures around them inform that their art and its relevance to societal analysis is not insignificant. Therefore the artistic expressions regarding women need not be looked upon as mere pictorial objects. They have the potential of showing up women's role as historical agents, and can reveal the range of constraints and opportunities women have had over time.

That the different countries of South Asia belong to a single cultural zone is a strong perception among both anthropologists and historians. While the inter-cultural and intra-cultural diversities among and within the countries of South Asia should form part of the present discourse, the overarching similarities across national boundaries can provide a common platform of understanding for "a shared vision". The language of art transcends state boundaries and has facilitated communication across diverse groups. Common myths and symbols are expressed through sculpture and painting despite stylistical variations encountered in different cultures. These motifs in art provide a common language of communication across South Asia.

In the case of the Sri Lankan experience, given the island's proximity to the subcontinent, relations between them have been necessarily close. While one is aware of instances of political tension between Sri Lanka and her South Indian neighbours, the harmonious pattern of cultural intercourse forms the most positive aspect of the Indian relationship. Looking back on these historical links, it is important to recognise that political conflict did not deter cultural cooperation and dialogue. This model of cultural exchange resulting in the spread of ideas, values and beliefs was the result of voluntary association and was not the result of political, or economic pressures exerted by the bigger neighbour. This is something one needs to emphasise. Much of the available evidence suggests that the cultural diffusion referred to was mostly a one way street. But Sri Lanka did pay her debts, for a reverse flow did take place in certain areas of art and religion. It is important to recognise that pre-colonial Asian cultures which received extraneous impulses selected certain cultural elements out of their own choice and in the context of Sri Lanka too there was this same selectivity. These elements were often restated in new terms and at times endowed with different meaning. One is not unaware of instances of cultural resistance when specific views did not conform to the host country's own ethos. In the evolution of any culture there is an inner dynamic at work which gives it a certain colour and texture. Therefore it is in the context of these basic interconnections and divergences that one has to clarify one's perceptions regarding the social position of women as represented in pre-modern Sri Lankan art.

Theoretical formations regarding women's status have to be tested against historical material and variables such as time, class and ethnicity have to be accounted for. In other words there is historical variability rather than uniformity in women's experience. Defining women is a shifting area in women's studies research and there is no single stance from which feminist scholars have viewed the experience of women. The patriarchal gender ideology which has become a bedrock of feminist scholarship has its critics and how the artist views power relations between the sexes can lead to a more nuanced approach which views the position of women in terms of constraints and opportunities they face.

With this introduction an attempt will be made to present some of the basic concepts outlined above.

Inter-Cultural Links

Writing on women in Indian art, Heinz Mode has said "...nowhere in the world than in India can women be entitled to claim higher rank than men in art, whether through the quantity of representations, the quality of their execution or the importance of their symbolic content" (Heinz Mode — *The Women in Indian Art,* New York) This concentration on the female figure in India is not matched by Sri Lanka and this is where the Buddhist ethos comes to play. Sri Lankan Art, especially its sculpture, is dominated by the Buddha image, and the female figure takes a back seat. This reticence is only true of Buddhist art in Sri Lanka, Hindu art follows the Indian genre. This is also true of the few representations we have of secular art.

A point which needs to be made and which is perhaps important in terms of diffusing current ethnic tensions, is the eclecticism of the Sri Lankan artists when it came to deriving inspiration from the different schools of Indian art. Numerous examples can be cited to demonstrate the fact that there was no regional bias in this regard.

The Social Position of Women as Depicted in Art

Symbolic Worship of Mother Earth

The issue of patriarchy and the subordination of women looms large in feminist discourse. Stereotypes of women as uniformly oppressed and unempowered do not provide us with a complete picture. On the positive side, motherhood is perhaps one of the most powerful concepts which pervades South Asian culture. The worship of the Mother Goddess has found visual expression from the earliest times in both India and Sri Lanka. The reproductive role of women associated with notions of fertility and good luck have elevated women to divine status. A common manifestation of the goddess dating back to as early as the 2nd century B.C. at Sanchi is the *Gajalakshmi* image. In Sri Lanka the image of *Lakshmi* as the goddess of good luck is represented in both Buddhist and Hindu art. The composition of *Lakshmi* bathed by elephants is even employed in secular structures as an auspicious symbol. This symbolic representation is very widespread in India too. The basic idea seems to be the pouring down of water over mother earth, making her fertile, the elephants representing rain clouds. Buddhists, Hindus and Jains, all of them seem to have internalised the veneration of *Lakshmi* within their own mythologies. It is very clear that this symbol of fertility is a manifestation of the Mother Goddess concept and forms a common substratum in the South Asian belief system.

The Concept of the Goddess and Her Cult Worship

The feminist view is that all religions are patriarchal. Religion either takes for granted male dominance or gives direct expression to it. As a general rule women occupy a subordinate status in most established religions. In *Theravada* Buddhism which is the dominant tradition in Sri Lanka, the Buddha is always male and there is no way in which a woman can become a Buddha. The *Mahayana* tradition, which has had a profound influence on Sri Lanka Buddhism, is somewhat more inclusive. The *Bodhisatva* or the aspiring Buddha can be either male or female, although according to some texts the female Bodhisatva becomes male at the point of Buddhahood. Sri Lankan Hinduism looks upon *Shiva* as the supreme god while *Vishnu* is accommodated more or less as a Buddhist god. Outside these formal structures dominated by the male, there is a strong undercurrent of goddess worship and often her mediation in human affairs has been much more powerful than that of the male gods.

Two of the most powerful goddesses worshipped in Sri Lanka today are *Pattini* and *Kali*. *Pattini* is a Buddhist goddess and is, in the popular imagination, the Compassionate Mother, warding off ill-health and other evils. She is also a *Bodhisatva* or a future Buddha, a notion which seems to have persisted in the popular mind from earlier times. The 8th and 9th centuries AD seem to have been the heyday of *Mahayana* Buddhism in Sri Lanka and the worship or *Tara* or the female *Bodhisatva* seems to have been very strong. Sometimes called *Pattini*, she is also the *Badhisatva Tara*. The unique image of Tara in transcendal meditation is a clear expression of the Buddhist view that women are capable of the highest spiritual attainment. Her cult worship was independent of the veneration of the male Bodhisatva.

The worship of goddess *Kali* has been mostly associated with Hinduism, but the cult has straddled the Hindu/Buddhist divide. *Durga* or *Kali* in the popular perception is the Great Goddess and there is no place for a supreme male god in some local belief systems, for instance in some parts of India. In the Hindu tradition, *Durga* is the warrior goddess, the *Sakti* or the counterpart of *Shiva*, not to be confused with his consort, *Parvati*. Her most powerful role is the destruction of evil and in this she takes on a very aggressive stance. There are many manifestations of the goddess, one where she stands on the head of a buffalo and another where she tramples evil, personified as a demon. More "benevolent" forms or "less war-like" forms of the goddess are widely seen in village temples in both India and Sri Lanka. The great reliance on the Mother Goddess through her many manifestations in both Hindu and Buddhist traditions represent a common value system which envelopes the whole South Asian region.

The Union of the Male/Female

The most logical evolution of the theory of *Sakti* is the depiction of the supreme God as both male and female — the *Ardhanari* form, half male and half female. A striking illustration of this concept as expressed in art is the image found at an excavation site at the Abhayagiri temple. Once again both the Buddhists and Hindus seem to have been comfortable with this idea, for numerous Indian examples can be cited in this regard. What is exemplified in these images is that the ultimate reality is both female and male.

The Representation of Women's Lives: Constraints and Opportunities

We have so far described the image of woman as the source of good fortune, the 'Great Mother' and the Supreme Goddess. While the artist has depicted all this, he also records for us the negative side, that women are controlled or subordinated. This is the contradiction that one faces regarding the social position of women as represented in art. Within the same tradition or the same belief system the two view points seem to coexist quite amicably.

Sita, exemplifies the Hindu wife, a perception which has wide ramifications throughout South Asian society. She is the divine consort whose sexuality is controlled. In both Buddhist and Hindu art, the goddess is most popularly represented as the consort of either the *Bodhisatva* or the main Hindu God. She is sometimes placed on a slightly lower plane as seen at the Vegiriya temple in Kandy and at the rock temple at Buduruvagale. Numerous examples can be cited in Hindu art; *Parvati* in the Cola tradition being one of the better examples.

The same phenomenon is seen among the lesser deities, the most extreme example that one can present is the guardian god at the Abhayagiri temple, whose consort is relegated to a small niche on the sculpted slab. However gender stereotyping can be quite problematic. The large number of guardian deities found in all parts of Sri Lanka (during all historical periods) is an eye-opener to the great variability in social attitudes towards women. As in the case of the principal deities, guardian deities are both male and female, the large number is of course male. Independent guardian goddesses are not uncommon, and one is also aware of the male/female guardians of equal stature. Therefore the relative importance of the consort in joint composition varies considerably. One needs to look at the possibility of changing attitudes over time and the perceptions of artists, patrons and donors for the interpretation of these artefacts. Radhika Coomaraswamy's statement that "women must be seen in context before she is seen in liberation" is perhaps very pertinent.

Women's Social and Political Roles

The pre-modern Sri Lankan artist has presented to us a wide repertoire of images reflecting women's social roles such as those of the dancer, the musician and the religious devotee. There is space in Asian culture for the talents of both men and women in dance and music without too much gender differentiation. However one can see a noticeable emphasis on the female dancer and very often the men provide the music, although the women do not always dance to their tune. Some Literary texts suggest that dancing and music were accomplishments which cut across class divisions but with time they appear to have been limited to the lower rungs of society. Here, it is the class bias rather than the gender bias that we seem to be confronted with. Parallels can be drawn from most South Asian cultures in this regard.

The religious devotee is a regular image among women represented in art. This is a position of power which has been assigned to women from very early times. However the mediatory role of women involving the divine is a private activity. The more prestigious role of mediation in the public sphere is assigned to men and the political influence of women is limited to the domestic arena.

The perception that informal networking among women is a source of power has been graphically demonstrated in a temple painting of the 17th century. Exchanging news and views around the village well is a familiar pre-occupation among women and an instance where the woman asserts herself, pushed by the village women is once again part of the same record.

Traditionally the political culture of South Asia did not provide adequate space for women to participate in the formal political arena. In Sri Lanka a few queens did reign but as a rule it was the men who wielded institutional power. Women were also completely shut out from official government positions. Although wives of kings were not part of the formal decision making structures, they did find opportunities to assume the role of power-brokers. A Jataka scene in a temple painting where the king confers with his ministers while the queen sits by his side sucking her infant child is to my mind a telling scene. This is not a ceremonial sitting of the king and queen with state officials. Although her domestic role is accentuated, the queen is not disinterested in the official decision-making process. A different interpretation of this scene is possible. That women have found indirect methods to gain power and influence demonstrate the lack of direct access to formal politics — a concern in most of South Asia.

It is not necessary to labour the point that painting and sculpture do not provide us with a complete picture of the position of women in pre-modern times. However they do furnish us with certain insights which can supplement and complement data derived from other sources, resulting in a much more holistic understanding of the status and roles of women in South Asian societies. Whether the strengths and weaknesses regarding the condition of women resonate across South Asia is the issue before this seminar.

PART IV

FUNDAMENTALISM & COMMUNALISM

Communalism and Religious Fundamentalism: Threat to Civilization

A.F. Salahuddin Ahmed

For any meaningful discussion on what we call communalism and fundamentalism, it would be worthwhile, I believe, to explain these terms in historical context of South Asia.

Communalism is a peculiar South Asian phenomenon. In the western countries they do not use the term in the sense we use it here. Communalism, in fact, does not signify any well-defined concept or doctrine. It is rather a state of mind or shall I say, somewhat perverted attitude nourished by individuals belonging to a particular religious community towards those belonging to other religious communities. It is a kind of tribal attitude born of hatred and fear with regard to other tribes. It, in fact, results from ignorance and misunderstanding created by various factors. Vested interests such as political, economic, religious and, in many countries specially of the so-called third world, military vested interests — these elements take advantage and exploit the situation to serve their nefarious ends.

What is known as fundamentalism, more precisely religious fundamentalism, stands for strict adherence to the letter and spirit, that is, fundamentals or fundamental tenets of religion in its prime or original classical form, of course as interpreted by its proponents. The fundamentalists blindly follow their faiths, are extremely intolerant of other faiths and are so de-humanized that they would not hesitate to kill and die for their cause. History tells us that such fundamentalist religious movements arise in societies passing through transition or facing some sort of challenge both from within and without.

The situation may be viewed in the context of the history of the Indian sub-continent. After Muslim conquest of northern India at the beginning of the 13th century, Hinduism faced a serious challenge from Islam. Unable to resist Muslims invasion, Hindu society sought to maintain its existence and strengthen its position from within by strengthening Hindu conservatism. The Hindu pundits of the time systematized the social and religious laws and tenets of Hinduism with pedantic thoroughness as defensive means against encroachment from outside. Thus emerged what may be called Hindu religious fundamentalism the progenitor of the present-day *Hindutva* as advocated by the *Viswa Hindu Parishad*, the BJP, the *Siv Sena*, the *Bajarangadal* and the like. These elements were responsible for the demolition of the historic Babri mosque which led to unprecedented communal disturbances in many parts of the sub-continent.

Now let us say something about Islamic religious fundamentalism. During the early and middle phase of Mughal rule particularly at the time of Akbar the Great (1556-1605) when the situation was very congenial for religious tolerance and eclectic ideas, a section of orthodox *ulama* whose chief spokesman was Sheikh Ahmad Sirhindi (1563-1625) initiated a revivalist movement which stood for strict adherence to the Islamic laws and institutions as propounded in the *Quran* and the *Sunnah* and fiercely opposed any compromise with Hinduism. During the early decades of the 19th century similar religious movements inspired by the Wahhabi movement in Arabia had taken place in northern India and Bengal. These were led by Sayyid Ahmad of Rae Barali and Titu Mir. Sayyid's movement was mainly religious and political; he died fighting *jihad* against the Sikhs. Titu's movement in West Bengal was religious and agrarian. While he aimed at purifying Muslim society, he fought against the oppression of the peasantry by Hindu Zamindars and European indigo planters and died a martyr. In East Bengal also a peasant leader Haji Shariatullah and his son Dudu Miyan had started similar movement namely *faraidi* movement which aimed at Islamizing the rural population. These movements failed because their leaders had little understanding of the realities of the situation prevailing in 19th century colonial India. Driven by blind religious faith they had sought vainly to solve contemporary social and economic problems by solutions of bygone days. In fact, such backward-looking movements only contributed to retarding the development of the Muslim community.

In our time the Jamat-e-Islami has emerged as a powerful Islamic fundamentalist party. It has built up strong base in Pakistan and Bangladesh. It is also active in India. Jamat's influence is largely noticeable in Afghanistan where the Talibans after capturing state power has succeeded in taking that country back to medieval barbarism. In fact, Islamic fundamentalism under different names now constitute serious threat to political and social order in many countries of Arab world particularly Algeria.

Today communalism and religious fundamentalism seem to threaten the fabric of our civilized existence. It is my firm conviction that only objective understanding of history can help us in withstanding this threat. Despite political divisions of 1947 and 1971 the people of the Indian sub-continent do share a common and, shall I say, indivisible cultural heritage. This heritage is the outcome of long and continuing process of intermixture and assimilation of indigenous and external elements. These elements have become inseparable from each other and have contributed to the making of our composite cultural tradition cutting across political barriers. Vested interests, both indigenous and foreign, have from time to time sought to destroy this unique tradition by sowing seeds of discord and conflict which had led to communal and sectarian violence bringing untold misery and suffering to the common people.

There is now a growing realization among all sections of people of the sub-continent, whether they are Indians, Pakistanis, Bengalis or Sri Lankans or Nepalese — that no major problem of any country could be solved by confrontation or conflict, that only through peaceful means, through mutual understanding, co-operation and goodwill, that all sources of discord could be removed.

History tells us that until the advent of British colonial rule, communal antagonism and violence as we have known in our time virtually did not exist. Relations between different religious communities were based largely on understanding and harmony. After the initial period of confrontation and conflict was over, the communities had learned from experience to live and let live. Political antagonism or war among the ruling circles did not affect the common people.

The people of the sub-continent are now tired of prolonged tension and conflict that have been raging in many parts of the region. They now want to live in peace which is essential for development and progress. Continuing tension in the sub-continent has led to arms build-up on an unprecedented scale. Each state is indulging in reckless military expenditure. This tends to weaken civil administration, the foundation of democratic government, and has, in some cases led to "militarization of the state". This could, as some social scientists have warned us, bring forth the nightmarish state of affairs such as the "brutalization of government and dehumanization of society". We must guard against such development at any cost.

FUNDAMENTALISM AND COMMUNALISM: SOME LITERARY RESPONSES

Anisuzzaman

I must confess at the beginning that I have some problem with the use of the word fundamentalism. As you know, the word was coined early in the century to identify a particular movement within Protestantism in the United States. In that sense of the term it is, perhaps, more applicable, in the case of the Muslims, to the Wahabi Movement in Arabia and the likes of them in India, such as the Tariqa-i-Muhammadiya and Faraidi Movement, which aimed at returning to the pristine purity of Islam and rejecting the later accretions as well as many innovations of modern science and technology. In common parlance, however, fundamentalism has gained currency to refer to the tendency of using religion for political purpose, antagonism to other faiths and their devotees and symbols, criticizing the Technical Age while accepting their benefits even when they are the products of followers of such religions that do not meet with their approval. I believe, we are using the word today in that connotation. Communalism, again, is a word that has gathered a special significance in the context of South Asia. An Englishman would understand it in the sense of something for common use or belonging to a community while in our usage it has a distinctly negative connotation: one who bears a grudge or hatred for members of other persuasion or persuasions. It is in this limited sense that we shall be using the word here. I should also add that the word secularism has also acquired a different denotation in this part of the world. In the west it stands for this worldliness and for separation of the church and the state. In South Asia, another concept has developed around the word: neutrality in respect of different religions or an equal treatment by the state of all faiths followed by its citizens.

Having said this, let us proceed to examine the reflections of fundamentalism and communalism in our literature. I believe, it would be quite in order to suggest that in Bengali literature, there are more references to communal harmony than to communal conflicts. It is doubtless that there were cleavages between one group of religionists and another, but there were also cleavages within the same religious group. For instance, there was a clear divide between the Hindu and the Muslim; the Hindus again, were divided by caste and the Muslim by their origin of descent, on the one hand, and by Shia-Sunni sectarianism on the other. Conflicts were there — between and within the communities — sometimes ideological, sometimes political and sometimes motivated by pure self-interest. During the first partition of Bengal in 1905 and the agitation for its annulment until 1911, Muslims and Hindus clashed in several places in Bengal. Rabindranath Tagore (1861-1941) looked into the depth of the problem and wrote a number of introspective essays. Such clashes took the form of communal riots in 1926 when Kazi Nazrul Islam (1899-1976) came up with moving essays and poems. The riots appeared in their ugliest face in 1946, and, then, in 1947, at the time of the partition of India. Those who clamoured for the partition of India and those who finally conceded to that demand hoped that it would put an end to communalism. That was not to be.

I have a feeling that Urdu has produced more creative writings on communal riots, particularly those of 1947, than Bengali, perhaps, because of the fact that the partition of the Punjab was accompanied by more bloodshed than that of Bengal. Similarly, it seems that West Bengal has produced more creative writings on the partition of Bengal than East Bengal, sometimes East Pakistan, and now Bangladesh, perhaps, because Bengalee refugees from East Bengal suffered more in the West than their counterparts from the West in the East.

In 1950 there were riots both in West and East Bengal. An anthology, *Dangar Panchti Galpa*, edited by Mustafa Nur-ul Islam (b. 1927) and Alauddin Al Azad (b. 1932), was published the same year. It included two short stories by Azad and Hasan Hafizur Rahman (1932-83), a one-act play by Munier Chowdhury (1925-71), and translations of two short stories by Krishan Chunder and Khwaja Ahmad Abbas. I wonder whether more were written at the time in East Bengal but was not collected and why translation of Urdu stories from India was preferred to original Bengali stories from the same country. Anyway, the slender volume recorded the misery of the common man and the triumph of humanity over the religious divide.

When the next riots took place in East Pakistan in 1964, all the newspapers carried the same editorial on the front page calling the Bengalee to resist the rioteers and most of the political leaders went out with the same appeal. The people responded. Amir Hossain Chowdhury, nephew of Rokeya Sakhawat Hossain, and a translator and writer in English, gave away his life to save a Hindu family in Dhaka. Such a positive response of the people may be seen as a cumulative effect of political and cultural movements that were taking place since 1950, and specially since the state language movement in 1952. A continuous campaign for communal harmony and secularism which became a part of such movements resulted in the founding of non-denominational students' organisations and political parties, opening the doors of the Awami League for non-Muslims, opposition to the nomenclature of the republic as Islamic and adoption of the principle of joint electorate for East Pakistan in the Constitution of 1956. With the flow of Bengalee nationalism, communalism had very little place in society.

Since 1964 no further communal disturbance took place in East Pakistan. It was during our war of liberation that Hindus became a special target of the Pakistan Army and communal propaganda was carried to its height by the state machinery, aided and abetted by communal political groups. Fictions on the war of liberation have not failed to take this fact into account.

The Constitution of Bangladesh, adopted in 1972, incorporated four fundamental principles of state policy: nationalism, socialism, democracy and secularism. Article 12 promised to eliminate communalism in all its forms and prohibited the abuse of religion for political purpose and Article 38, *inter alia*, prevented people from forming political organizations on communal basis.

Following the killing of Bangabandhu Sheikh Mujibur Rahman, that part of Article 38 was removed from the Constitution in May 1976 and, six months later, Article 12 was deleted — both under Proclamation Orders issued under the Martial Law. These enabled the religion-based parties to stage a comeback and the communalists to carry on their propaganda afresh in the name of Islam. A Dhaka newspaper, belonging to one of the worst offenders of 1971, carried a news item on 31 October 1990 that the Babri mosque has been destroyed. It sparked off communal disturbances in many places in Bangladesh — Chittagong and Dhaka being the most affected ones. The resistance, spontaneous but ill-organized, came mostly from non-government quarters. When the Babri mosque was actually demolished in December 1992, the scale of atrocities in Bangladesh was much higher. Churches and Buddhist temples were also reported to have come under attack. The people resisted at places and the administration moved at some other, but the loss of confidence on the part of the non-Muslin population in Bangladesh was irreparable.

The writers played their part. Akhtar Hussain (b. 1945) edited *Sampradayikata-birodhi Galpa* (Dhaka, 1991) in which 11 short stories in Bengali (eight by Showkat Osman (b. 1917), Syed Waliullah (1922-71), Ishaq Chakhari (1922-?), Abu Ishaq (b. 1926), Sucharit Chowdhury (1929-94), Hasan Hafizur Rahman, Alauddin Al Azad and Hasan Azizul Huq (b. 1939) from Bangladesh and three from West Bengal by Ramesh Chandra Sen, Samaresh Basu and Salil Chowdhury), three from Urdu (those by Sadat Hosain Manto, Khwaja Ahmad Abbas and Krishan Chunder), two from Hindi (by Yashpal and Rangeya Ragho) and two from Punjabi (by Bhisma Sahabi and Kulwant Singh Viru) were collected. Many of these stories were written much earlier, but the anthology was meaningful in the context because it brought out the similarity both in the communal situation and the writers' responses in the three countries of India, Pakistan and Bangladesh.

1992 produced more. Shafi Ahmed and Purabi Basu edited *Ekhono Galo Na Andhar* (Dhaka, 1993) which collected all the articles, editorials, post-editorials and letters to the editors published in the Dhaka press between 7 and 13 December 1992, on the subject of communalism. It also included some poems and stories most of which were written contemporaneously. Mafidul Huq from Dhaka and Arun Sen from Calcutta jointly edited *Dhvangsasastupe Alo/Babri Masjid-Rammandir Vivad* (Dhaka and Calcutta, 1993) a compilation of anti-communal writings published in the Dhaka and Calcutta press, following the demolition of the Babri mosque.

I have already mentioned some of the writers of Bangladesh who have responded to the communal situation. To this list must be added the names of Ahmed Sharif (b. 1921), Kabir Chowdhury (b. 1923), Ataur Rahman (b. 1927), Mahbub-ul-Alam Chowdhury (b. 1927), Ajoy Roy (b. 1928), Zillur Rahman Siddiqui (b. 1928), Mazharul Islam (b. 1928), Shamsur Rahman (b. 1929), Badruddin Umar (b. 1931), Faiz Ahmed, Syed Atiqullah (b. 1933), Shamsuzzaman Khan (b. 1937), Hasnat Abdul Hye (b. 1939), Hayat Mamud (b. 1939), Rabiul Hassain (b. 1943), Mahadev Saha (b. 1944), Nirmalendu Gun (b. 1945), Syed Manzoorul Islam (b. 1951), Rabindra Gop (b. 1951), Sushanta Majumdar (b. 1954) and Taslima Nasreen (b. 1962).

Shamsur Rahman, our foremost poet, produced some remarkable poems, both in 1990 and 1992. He proclaims that non-Muslims shall not leave their home and hearth — a sentiment echoed in Sushanta Majumdar's story. Like Rahman, Mahadev Saha calls man a biped animal and is full of self-reproach for his misdeeds. Nirmalendu Gun reminds his readers that while a Hindu does not take beef and a Muslim abhors the flesh of a he-goat, the butcher kills both the animals with the same knife. Taslima Nasreen has created a lot of controversy over her novel, *Lajja* (1993). Although as a novel it is weak, Nasreen has good reasons to be indignant and that she expresses in several forms of writings. Hasnat Abdul Hye wrote three exceptional stories, two of which are now collected in his *Sreshtha Galpa* (Dhaka, 1994). In one, the characters have no name; they could have been members of the minority community anywhere in the world. No greater harm is done to them except that a missile thrown from outside breaks the window-pane of their home. But the fact that the main character is asked to stay home and not to attend office, assured that he is safe, inquired after his well-being — all on a particular day on which the processionists and the police chase each other alienates him totally. In the other story, the Headmaster's daughter is kidnapped on the eve of her wedding. The father asks almost everyone to help trace her. And when she returns home after three days in a dishevelled state, the headmaster can only whisper: 'why did you have to come back, my child?'

The father in the story is however not alone in his anguish. The writers in Bangladesh share his burden and Shamsur Rahman, again, says:

> I do not have enough tears in my eyes
> That I can put out that terrible fire.
> I do not have enough room on my writing desk
> That I can accommodate
> The hundreds of men pursued by those cannibals.
>
> The words that were coming to me —
> Fluttering like butterflies,
> Swimming like fishes,
> Like a shining current of stars,
> Like buzzing bees —
> They are now burning in a terrible conflagration.

(Translated by Kabir Chowdhury)

It is not the rioters alone that our writers have been confronting. In the countryside, the Imams of local mosques and the head Mudarris of Madrasas have, for sometime, started playing the role of protectors of public morality. In several cases, they have accused women, in particular, of immorality and sentenced them to stoning for a period of time or to suffer a specific number of lashes on their body. In one case a girl died of the punishment and in another she committed suicide for such humiliation. Many writers have voiced protest and Imdadul Huq Milan is writing a two volume novel after the suicide's name, *Nurjahan*, of which one volume (Dhaka, 1995) has come out. In the cities several writers like Sufia Kamal, Ahmed Sharif, Kabir Chowdhury, Shamsur Rahman, Faiz Ahmed and Taslima Nasreen (and an artist of the late Qamrul Hasan's eminence) have been declared *murtad* or apostates by some religion political groups and rewards have been publicly declared for their heads. Taslima Nasreen is now self-exiled in Europe.

The same groups are clamouring to declare the Ahmadiyas and the Shias non-Muslims. Systematic attacks have been made on the Ahmadiya centres, mosques and homes. Without entering into the religious debates, most of our writers have deplored these attempts at dividing the people, these demonstrations of intolerance, and these violations of rights, norms and civilities. It is not enough for a writer in Bangladesh to respond to fundamentalism and communalism through his writings, the circumstances demand him to turn an activist as well.

MUSLIMS AND I

Vijay Tendulkar

I was born in 1928 in Mumbai in a Maharashtrian middle class family.

Mumbai was known and spoken of, except in Marathi speaking families of Maharashtra, as Bombay.

Even those Marathi speaking gentlemen who had higher education — which had its accent on English — and wished to show their proficiency in the language of the rulers, would fondly call the city Bombay.

Bombay was fashionable with us; Mumbai was natural. And of course the original. It was turned into Bombay by the white sahibs first and then by the brown sahibs as was the practice.

Mumbai of that time was not as sprawling and overcrowded as it is to-day. The city was limited to its core area which was sparsely populated. You could walk on the road at any time of the day without being bumped off by a speeding vehicle or colliding with another pedestrian rushing to reach somewhere. Life even with clocks and watches was long enough to be enjoyed with its simple comforts and to be lived without the persistent feeling of anxiety.

We still had to learn by heart and recite a poem eulogising George the Fifth, the then emperor of the British Empire, on which the sun never set. This poem was a part of our school curriculum. At the same time the air outside was charged with Mahatma Gandhi's movements of non-violence and the memories of Lokamanya Tilak and Shahid Bhagat Singh which were still very fresh in the minds of the elders. My mother, who was a housewife and was barely educated as most women of that time used to be, talked fondly of the meetings she had attended of Tilak and his powerful oratory and the terrible night on which Bhagat Singh was hanged. 'Bhagat Singh! Hai Hai!' She would tell us how these muffled slogans of the mourners echoed on the roads of Mumbai through that night. My college-going elder brother was already in the freedom movement and had pledged himself to *swadeshi* and *charkha*, the spinning wheel that Gandhi had turned into a household item.

Once in a while the atmosphere would suddenly get tense, everyone looked concerned, I was urgently brought home from the nearby school and my elder brother who had grown a beard was pressurised to shave it off for the time being. This meant that a communal riot had begun in the city.

Hindus shed any resemblance to a Muslim and took extra care to look a thorough Hindu and made it a point to avoid Muslim localities till things got normalised again. They in their routine existence had very little to do in these localities except passing through them in a tram or a bus toward another destination. It was an alien part of the city for them; segregated in their psyche like the prostitutes' area. One avoided even passing through this Muslim area for safety's sake till the end of the tensions between the two communities (names were meticulously avoided in the media) were officially over. Withdrawal of the curfew was a sure sign of the situation returning to normal.

There was no way to know what happened to the Muslims in the city during the riot situation; but even I, a child, would hear about incidents in which a Muslim hawker or a beggar who strayed into the Hindu locality was promptly stabbed in the back or in the belly. A similar incident of a lone Hindu straying into the Muslim locality and getting stabbed was as a rule mentioned after such an incident in the Hindu locality was narrated. May be to convince the listeners — and the narrator himself — that it was only in the fitness of things; a case of squaring off the account or a case of tit for tat which was perfectly justified.

But I clearly remember; there would be a short or long hush in the conversation before this topic was resumed or changed.

The hush was not out of a feeling of doubt about the wisdom of such a justification but probably the white-collared clerics and their families felt uncomfortable with even the verbal feel of bloody violence. They had got so used to the smooth working of the Law and Order machinery of the British Raj and the peaceful existence of the politically uninvolved middle class under it.

Truly life then was paradise for my family and for families like mine as compared to the routine gang wars and the murders and the decoities committed in the white-collared middle class localities of Mumbai now. And the much publicised complicity of the police in such terrible happenings. One would not even dream of such complicity then. Not only the police but the government machinery as a whole was taken to be above board in its functioning. Whether it was, is anybody's guess.

Going back to the topic of my paper, I did not get an opportunity to meet my first Muslim or even to see one — a real one — from near till I was well over twelve years old. Not many of my class, i.e., the white-collared middle class — even in their adult age — got this opportunity of meeting a real Muslim in person in their normal life in a so-called cosmopolitan city of Mumbai. One was only aware of a Muslim existence in another part of the city and inherited some stray ideas about them while he or she grew into an adult.

What were the ideas like?

Let me recount from my experience.

A Muslim meant someone with a beard. It also meant an unclean appearance; even an uncouth behaviour lacking education and culture. Someone you better stay away from. Contact in any form was supposed to be dangerous. I still remember a common expression very frequently heard in casual conversations of the white-collared adults: (माणूस आहेस का मुसलमान ?) Are you a human being or a Muslim? It was never said seriously; the tone would be light; half-joking; even frivolous. Casual. Once it was said in my class by my teacher to one of the troublesome students. The student did not mind it. He grinned sheepishly as it was said. No one seemed to mind in fact. It was a way of saying your behaviour is most unseemly.

My first education on the Muslims began with historical plays of the time. Those plays invariably dealt with the ascendance of Shivaji the Maratha king who freed the Hindus of Maharashtra from the Mughal rule and established his own rule which came to be known as the *Hindu-pada-padshahi*, i.e., the empire of the Hindus. The first such play I saw had Shivaji's son Sambhaji as the hero, who according to the history of that time was a passionate womaniser and an alcoholic and a generally irresponsible young man who preferred a martyr's death in Mughal Emperor Aurangzeb's prison to getting converted to Islam. It was staged in our school as part of the annual day function. All the actors were school children (older than me) and they were directed by one of our teachers. The play had been originally written for adults and had earned an acclaim on the commercial stage. Like any Marathi historical play of those days this too had the Mughal emperor Aurangzeb, Shivaji's arch-rival in his fight against the tyrannies of the Muslim religious fanatics against the Hindus, as the bad man of the play. He was painted in loud colours; a religious fanatic, a ruthless tyrant, a despicable figure with a long white beard on a crooked face wearing garish costumes and shouting swearwords supposedly form Urdu and Farsi (I did not understand them but felt very piqued by them:) directed at Shivaji's son and the ruling Maratha Emperor Sambhaji and his men. In short he was like the villain in any commercial Hindi *massala* film of to-day. Alternately comic and repulsive. The rest of the Mughal characters in the play were drunkards, lechers, capable of any dastardly act and big-mouthed cowards who always lost in a fight with Sambhaji's brave little men. (*mavlas*, the Maratha soldiers were small in stature.)

The Maratha *Mavlas* stood in contrast to these Mughal ruffians and buffoons. All the applause-winning dialogue was given to Sambhaji and his men by the playwright and the 'enemy camp' pouted only hatred toward the *kafir* Marathas, toward their 'holy' cows and contempt toward the Hindu religion on the whole.

As children we were made to participate in and watch many such baffling (baffling for us children) specimens of adult theatre; this was only one of them. The very first I watched and brooded over for days.

You can imagine my reaction at that age to this mind-blowing theatre experience.

Being a school production the audience, in addition to me, was of mainly children of the age-group between six to sixteen.

Apart from this our school text books carried excerpts from Marathi historical plays which shaped our ideas of our past and also the present to a large extent. Access to authentic history at that age is out of the question. Even if one finds an access at a later age the ideas — some of them weird and twisted — are already formed at an early age and though they *can* change over a time I doubt whether they disappear entirely from one's psyche. Our attitudes have a lot to do with what we internalise in our early formative years.

The first real Muslim in my life was a boy in my class. This was after we left Mumbai for Kolhapur, a small town at that time. My new school had boys from lower castes who were the sons of lorry-drivers, tailors, carpenters and we had a girl in our class who was the daughter of a 'kept woman' or a concubine of a rich man — a novelty even for the more knowledgeable among us. I met Sheikh here in the school. On the first day of the school we were made to stand up one by one and say 'present sir' as our class teacher read out the roll-call. When a tall, gaunt boy with high cheek bones and small peering eyes answered to the name of Hussein Ali Izaz Ali Sheikh (the first and the second name is my imagination; since I do not remember the original ones;) I looked twice, with utter disbelief at that boy wearing a home-washed pajama, a neat cotton coat fully buttoned on a clean white home-washed shirt and a black shapeless cap properly placed on his head through which his unruly hair sprouted out from all sides.

I simply could not believe my eyes. He did not fit into the concept of a Muslim in my mind at all. He was like any boy. He was so gentle and shy and soft-spoken in spite of looking bigger than us! And he did not utter any swear-words. As the days passed I also found that Sheikh was a studious boy, he spoke my language, i.e., Marathi — though later I found that it had a natural mix of Urdu (not of the Aurangzeb kind) when he was away from the school especially at his home and with his family — and this mix of Urdu and Marathi sounded sweeter than my chaste Marathi. And Sheikh was very sociable. Warm in his general behaviour. Eager to make friends. Very co-operative. When I was unwell and had to stay away from the class. Sheikh would help me in catching up with the back-log by offering me his note-books. We became friends despite my deep-rooted reservations about his being a Muslim. He lived in a locality which was in the same direction as mine. He had to walk farther on. So we left school together every evening. Chatted on the way. For days I could not make up my mind on whether I should invite him home or not. He was a Muslim after all. Besides my own reservations about the Muslims I had apprehensions about how Sheikh will be received by others at home. I had even avoided mentioning our friendship to my parents. One day during the lunch break he offered me something from his lunch box. I had not thought of doing so. I ate from my box and he from his though we ate sitting on the same school bench. That day when he took out something from his lunch box and held it in front of me I dithered. I did not know whether I should eat from a Muslim's lunch box. I did since I could not say no to Sheikh but my conscience troubled me that night for doing what I had done. I even imagined in my sleep that I had turned into a Muslim and my family was blaming me for eating from a Muslim's lunch box. 'Good for you!' They were saying in a chorus. 'Want to eat from a Muslim, eh?' And my mother was crying her heart out for my becoming a Muslim.

But soon this feeling of guilt disappeared and I even invited Sheikh to my house one day to see my collection of kites. I did not inform my family about the religion of my school friend but they discovered it while Sheikh was at our house. Probably by Sheikh's way of speaking or his appearance. I do not know how. To my surprise they did not object. My mother took care to tell me that night not to go to his house and not to be 'very friendly' with him. 'He seems to be a good boy' she said, 'but these people (she meant the Muslims) are not our kind. It is better to stay away from them.'

If I remember correctly, he was uncomfortable and tense for a while in his first visit to my house but liked the house and my family and then frequently came to my house to play with me.

His father was a butcher by profession. I did not know this for months. Nor did my family with their vegetarian habits knew;

otherwise I would have been forbidden from mixing with Sheikh. I myself came to know it when I was compelled to go to his house for the first time when I learned that Sheikh was not well and would not be able to come to the school for some time. After knowing this I wanted to help him in his back-log of studies. So I decided after some inner resistance that I shall go to his house. I remember the shock I felt after meeting his father. He was a typical village Muslim in appearance as in his manners; warm, natural, robust yet gentle and in a coloured *lungi* and white *kurta*. He was curious about me and my upper-caste Hindu family. He had seen and even met Hindus but only as clients who came to his shop to buy mutton. He had no qualms about his profession. He talked about it as casually as my father did about his clerical profession. My father talked of files and paper; Sheikh's father talked of the quality of the mutton he sold and the intestines and brain and the liver of the sheep he killed. His gentle nature never matched with his 'violent' profession in my mind. How can he kill the poor animals and be so gentle? I used to ask myself in those days. Years after that I became a flesh-eater and never cared to ask myself how I relish eating animals killed by someone, with the gentle, non-violent nature I have.

Sheikh's mother and sister kept themselves in the kitchen when men — even I — were around. They wore *burkhas* and looked mysterious and even sinister to my eyes because of that. I had not seen anyone in a *burkha* till then. Not even in a Marathi historical play. I could not imagine my mother or my sister moving in our house in a *burkha*.

Sheikh's mother called me 'beta' and gave me some sweet dish to eat. I had not eaten anything as tasty as that in my life or I thought so while I ate the 'special' dish.

Sheikh was not keen to show me his father's shop. I insisted out of curiosity that he should take me there only once. I went with him and could not take in the gory sight of raw headless cadavers hanging upside down. It upset my stomach and I even felt that I shall throw up but managed not to. That first sight of raw flesh and blood was so irresistable to me in spite of the revulsion I experienced that I wanted to visit that shop again and see a sheep being killed by Sheikh's father. For some reason Sheikh avoided it.

May be he himself did not like his father's profession. Or he did not relish killing.

My friendship with Sheikh was my first genuine education on the subject of Muslims. Sheikh remained behind when we left Kolhapur for Pune, a predominantly Brahmin city at that time. It was nearly impossible to get an accommodation in a Brahmin locality of Pune if you were — no, not a Muslim — a non-Brahmin. You would be asked to state your caste before anything else was discussed and we were non-Brahmins. Which meant that we were 'flesh-eaters'. In fact my family was strictly vegetarian but it took a lot of effort for my father to get a place for us in a decent 'no-flesh' locality.

The next crucial influence in my life *vis-a-vis* the Muslims was the experience of partition of the country. We were given to understand — and we readily believed — that Mohmmad Ali Jinnah was the villain of the piece in this gory drama that unfolded before us mostly through the media and all kinds of hearsay. Even the most authentic accounts of the massacres that took place in this period on both sides of the deviding line read like cheap pulp fiction consisting of unlimited violence and the most pervert kind of sex. For us Jinnah was the cause of it all. And his Muslim League of-course. The word Muslim had a familiar connotation for us. It meant uncultured, illiterate, undeveloped minds full of perversities and a violent drive always ready to go berserk. And Hindus though cultured and civilised had no option but to retaliate with the same pervert violence.

I was in my late teens then.

When we heard on the radio that Gandhi has been assassinated everyone around me knew for certain — and made no bones of it — that the assassin had to be a Muslim. When we were told that he was not a Muslim but a Hindu our minds in spite of their benumbed state refused to believe it. But then we knew why a Hindu had to kill the Mahatma. Because of the pro-Muslim politics of the otherwise great man. Politics which pampered the wicked Muslims at the cost of the interests of the well-behaved, gentle Hindus.

Those were the days of a rabid anti-Muslim feeling around me.

This is when I heard a new Marathi word for the first time. It was not new in that sense. I had heard and even used it before. The word was (लांड्या). Its literal meaning was 'an animal whose tail has been cut'. Generally a dog. When I heard it for the first time in a new context — to suggest a Muslim — I could not catch its new meaning. Then I was enlightened on this subject by friends. And soon I tried to use it in my speech and felt very self-conscious; even embarrassed. But that word became a household word during those days even among the boys of my age. The bias which had been intentionally and unintentionally sown in our minds when we were children now grew into a confirmed opinion. Muslims were an aggressive rowdy savage rabid minority: dogs with a cut tail; their leaders used them for their gains; and the secular Hindu leaders like fools were playing in their hands at the cost of the interests of us Hindus who were a majority but suffered at the hands of a mere minority.

I too held this view though not with the fanatic anger of the typical white-collared Hindu of that time.

In this very period another Muslim entered my life. He was leading the cultural squad of the undivided Communist Party in my state. He was Amar Sheikh. *Shaheer* (the bard) Amar Sheikh as he was widely known. He came from a poor rural Muslim family and sang songs with a political message.

His voice was a musical but strong booming voice which thrilled an audience of thousands by its thunder. It was not necessary to be a communist to feel charged by it's magic. The 'revolutionary' message did not mar the lilt and the roar of the singing. I came under the irresistible charm of this voice so much so that the fact that the singer was a Muslim or did not bother me even in that climate full of anti-Muslim feelings. The songs moved me as if they came straight from the heart. Once in a while I did wonder how a Sheikh, a Muslim, could put so much passion in some of the patriotic songs he sang. But his style of singing them was irresistable. I began singing those songs imitating his style. I would stand like him. Upright and chaste thrown out; then sing imagining myself to be him. (My fair complexion could not match his tan black and he was too manly in looks as compared to my vegetarian adolescent looks — which gave me a terrible complex.) I was in my late teens now and still with the bias against Muslims in general and an ardent fan of a Muslim: Shaheer Amar Sheikh.

We became friends after many years and remained friends till he died in an accident.

Incidentally I came to know about his mother after he died. Munerbi, Amar Sheikh's mother, was an illiterate Muslim woman married to a small farmer and a poetess of unusual strength. The poems she composed had a natural mix — a captivating intermingling — of both, the Muslim and the Hindu cult. The imagery came straight from the Bhakti poets and the poems flowed from Urdu into Marathi and back to Urdu like a child frolicking between two sections of a house divided by a recently erected wall. At times the meter is traditional Marathi, used by the Bhakti saints and the language Urdu as spoken by the rural Muslims in Maharashtra. In one of her poems she sees Krishna, the Hindu God, in her Muslim son.

In 1967 her Muslim son, the bard Amar Sheikh, poses a question to his readers in an article: How am I a traitor? He narrates a happening: 'I cannot forget that day. I had returned from an election meeting in which I had performed as usual and was taking a nap when I was awakened by some commotion. Then a kick on the door of my apartment in the chawl. Then another kick. The door gave way with it. It opened wide. Someone rushed in. Lunged at me. I sprang to my feet and grabbed him. A battle royal ensued. My attacker was in his early thirties. I had completed fifty. I did not spare him. Nor did he while letting himself go at me. It is not the beating I had to take that hurts; but the words which he shouted at me. The mind behind those words. 'Amar Sheikh is a Muslim' he yelled. 'He deserves to be lynched. He has married a Hindu woman. Haul me before a court and put me in a jail but I shall come out and lynch this man. I shall become a martyr for killing a Muslim.'

Amar Sheikh writes further in this article: 'I have been living in this locality for the last seven years. My attacker grew up watching me. My daughter grew up with him. And to-day he barges into my house after beating up three Muslims on his way. Why? Because I am a Muslim. And a Muslim is a traitor; an arch-enemy of this country. I with my record of service to this country and to my people am called a traitor and he who has never shown any concern for this country is a patriot because he is born a Hindu! We were born as

Muslims and that puts a stamp on our forehead in this country: TRAITOR! Why?'

This excerpt says everything.

I came across Munerbi's poetry and this article of her son in a book which was given to me during the post Babri-masjid days, i.e., when the communal passions were running high once more in the country and a spate of communal riots was already on. The climate around me was once again ripe with Muslim — hating and the word I had heard again for years after I had heard it first during the partition of the country: (**लांड्या**). The human dog with a cut tail.

The answer to Amar Sheikh's question immediately came to my mind.

Because we were brought up that way. We, the Hindu children; with casual remarks like (माणूस आहेस का मुसलमान)? Are you a human being or a Muslim? Because of our grooming which prohibited and taught us to shun any contact with Muslims. Because of the biases knowingly and unknowingly sown in our minds by displaying and teaching our history (in my case the Mughal and Maratha period of it) in a wrong light. Because of the experience of the partition of the country as felt through the media and of the preceding years of Hindu-Muslim relations as they percolated to us through the attitudes of the elders. But most of all because of the **total lack of contact**, a wide chasm between us and the Muslims among us, as people.

Yes, I am aware of the games the politicians played among both the communities from time to time and the communal passions whipped up by them to suite their politics of self-interest based on hatred. But those games would not have succeeded to the extent they did if we Hindus and the Muslims had known each other better; if we had grown together from our childhood as one community than two separate worlds within one nation.

After Amar Sheikh I had the good fortune of having Hameed Dalvai the Muslim reformer of the sixties in my life. We became friends much before he plunged into the Muslim reform movement. He was a creative writer. He wrote short stories. I was the editors of the monthly magazine in which one of the first readers of his writing. He wrote about his community. His childhood. He wrote with anguish about his mother who was the third wife of his father. About communal riots. He wrote with a searing insight about his community, the Muslims.

Those were my real lessons in understanding the Muslims in my society. My days with Hameed. The working of the minds of the Muslims, their up-bringing, what they were taught about us, the Hindus, in their early formative years and the biases they were injected with at an early age. All this realization came through Hameed. Through our long evenings and nights of intimate conversations.

Hameed had come to learn about my Hindu world more of less in the same way as I came to learn about his: through whatever little contact we could make with the 'other' world, the other side of the communal divide, by going out of our way in our adolescent years to know things by ourselves. His father was a Muslim Leaguer. A local leader of the League and a Hindu-hater. Hameed had grown up as a boy in this political climate. He grew out of it in later years. In his young age.

When he worked for a better understanding between the two communities and progressive social reforms in his own community particularly concerning the state of Muslim women, he was branded a traitor and a heretic by the majority of his people — especially the diehard conservative men of his community; and was simultaneously looked at as an exception and a freak within his Muslim community by the Hindu intelligentsia.

One of our writers who proudly proclaimed himself as a Hindu revivalist once advised Hameed — and with genuine concern — 'You will always be an outsider among the Muslims. Why don't you become a Hindu? After all your forefathers were Hindu. You have Hindu blood in your vains. Come, I shall arrange for your conversion to Hindudom.'

Hamid laughed heartily every time he heard this. But he did say to me once in his introspective mood: 'We The Indian Muslims are a peculiar lot. Our forefathers did not come from across the borders of the country. They were not the invaders but the invaded like the Hindus. They were Hindus. They were converted to Islam mostly under pressure; even by force. If this is true, then we belong here. We have Hindu genes in our system and a Muslim upbringing, a Muslim bias. We are a product of a mixed or hybrid culture which makes us an isolated lot; removed from the general reality, the general ethos. We belong no where. Not to the Muslim world outside nor to the predominantly Hindu world of this country. We have no roots to claim. And our loyalties will always remain questionable in this country. Not necessarily because of what we do but because of what we are expected to do — as an alien race whose interests lie outside of this country. It will be presumed that we do it, that we have done it though we may have not. And we must not. Whatever happens to this country happens to us. Our fate is tied up to the fate of this society which may never accept us as its natural integral part.'

Hameed died prematurely of kidney failure.

After him I have had many Muslim friends. Some of them mean much more than friends to me. But when I look back at our friendship I find a subtle difference between them and my other — I mean Hindu — friends.

I meet a Hindu friend and am never conscious of his religion. He is just a friend. But when I meet a Muslim friend I never forget, never can forget, that he is a Muslim. If I forget this for a brief time my upbringing reminds me that he is Muslim. I am proud of his friendship. I love him more for that.

Ideally it should be no less, no more.

A friendship is beyond *all* considerations. Is it not?

IDEALS OF HUMANISM AND CO-EXISTENCE IN PAKISTANI LITERATURE

Intazir Husain

Let me first narrate a Muslim mystics dream as told by him to his disciples. One night during his wanderings in Hardware he saw in his dream two grand Darbars arranged on the two sides of the Ganges, one headed by Sri Krishnji, the other by Prophet Muhammad (peace be upon him). He found himself loitering in the vicinity of the Darbar of Sri Krishn, who spotted him and referred his case to the Prophet (peace be upon him). 'I leave it to you to instruct him,' came the reply from the Prophet. So Sri Krishnji called him out and said 'Moorakh, what are you searching here. Go back to the Darbar you have come from. You will find these all you are in search of.'

The dream has been narrated in Tazkar-ai-Ghousia, a collection of what the disciples heard from his murshad Syed Ghous Ali Shah, a Nineteenth century mystic living in Panipath. The dream, I think, symbolizes the collective dream seen by the saints and the sufis of South Asia in the past centuries. It was this collective dream which had inspired the Bhakti movement with Kabir as its great exponent, who was soon followed by Guru Nanak, Dadu, and a number of such other saints and saint poets.

This dream or the ideal of humanism and peaceful co-existence of faiths and creeds as envisaged by the sufis, the saints, and the saint poets, though never realized at any stage of history, did not go in vain. Through their teachings and their devotional poetry, it travelled far and wide and deeply influenced literary traditions of different languages in the South Asia. It is for the scholars and researchers to determine the extent of this influence. I with my limitations as a student of literature can, however, discern it in the literary tradition I am associated with. This discernment encourages me to assert that the new humanistic trends with their emphasis on social justice and woman emancipation, which inform the present writings in Pakistan, can be traced back to this influence.

One may define these trends as the outcome of the progressive movement, which for decades has been a dominant influence in our literature, and of the Western literature, which with its secular values has been a constant influence with us. And as contemporary literature in other South Asian countries too has been under these influences, so one may conclude that the traces of shared values we find in the different literary traditions of South Asia at present owe their origin to these two sources. I will not deny these influences nor will try to minimize their extent. However, I will insist that not withstanding these immediate influences, these trends have deeper roots. They get their nourishment from the age-old literary tradition steeped deep in the ideas and ideals emanating from the inspired teachings of the saints and their *sufis*. In case of Urdu, we see this influence permeating poetry from its very start.

Quli Qutab Shah, who ruled over the kingdom of Golconda, is counted among the earliest poets of Urdu. The poet in him surpassed the ruler. And he was a kind of poet, who refused to recognize the distinctions on the basis of religious faith. 'I am bothered neither about the temple nor about the mosque' so he said in a couplet.

The secular tone set by Quli Qutab Shah was to be followed by those who came after him. In consequence to that the whole tradition of Urdu ghazal is steeped in secular values. The reason for it perhaps lies in a constant situation in the Indo-Muslim society, where we see a continuous tug of war between two forces opposed to each other, say orthodoxy as against the human spirit pining for free expression and its consummation in the experience of love. This tussle is best reflected in our classical ghazal, where Majnoon, the lover and Mansoor, the mystic emerge as two potent symbols upholding the values of love, liberal thinking, and freedom of expression as against

Sheikh, Zahid (the pious man), Waiz (the preacher) and Mohatsib (the censoring authority), who all symbolize orthodoxy and stand condemned for their obscurantism.

And here is Attiya Dawood, who writes in Sindh:

Mother, this latch on the door
You were told to keep it locked
From the inside
Open it now.
Otherwise I have become tall enough
To reach out to it.

Such is the temper of the feminine protest poetry, a protest borders on rebellion. For this temper it is indebted to the Movement of Women Liberation, which has made Pakistani Women acutely conscious of their repressed conditions. Now the Pakistani female writers have a cause to fight for and a theme to write about. I, however, feel tempered to trace the origin of this trend in Sir Syed's movement, whose distinguished writers like Maulana Hali and Deputy Nazir Ahmad were writing about the pathetic conditions of women in our society and were pleading for female education.

The female education has brought an awakening in its wake. Women in our society no more stand in need of a Maulana Hali or a deputy Nazir Ahmad to plead their case. Thanks to their education and to influences such as of women liberation movement, they have gained confidence to fight themselves for their rights as they have conceived them in contradiction with the early reformers moderate concept of women rights, which may now appear to them smacking of conservation. So female poetry and fiction in Pakistan appear at present to be a kind of war front against male domination, a battle for the emancipation of women.

While speaking of fiction in particular I feel tempted to refer to the short stories and novels written in the early years of Pakistan as they carry with them a humanitarianism tone, which in times to come was to assimilate by Pakistani fiction and grow as an integral part of its tradition. Writers in these stories are generally seen trying to be objective and dispassionate in their depiction of the riot ridden conditions in those days, an attempt to stick to sanity amidst collective insanity. This fiction may be read as a search for human values lost in the holocaust of Partition. Here we find story writers rising above prevalent prejudices and seeing things in a wider humanitarian perspective. Their humanitarianism prompts them to make a search for what is humane in people gone insane under the influence of communal frenzy. The search in most cases leads to the discovery of a good soul stick to the values of love, and amity as against the communal hatred rising high all around him. One such good soul is Dauji, a Hindu character, so nicely portrayed by Ashfaq Ahmad, in his story Gadariya (The shepherd). Dauji, a teacher with a mystical bent of mind, refuses to be swayed by the general trend of migrating to India and stays calmly where he is. But the rioters are not going to spare him. In his last moments he appears to a Muslim student, who is a narrator in this story, a Saint in the true sense.

In the different stories by Pakistani writers like Ahmad Nadeem, Qasmi A. Hameed, Jamila Hashmi and so many others, we may easily trace this kind of trend. As for Manto, I will better quote Mohammad Hasan Askari, a distinguished critic in Urdu, who while discussing riot fiction said that Manto appears saying that man in spite of all in human acts perpetrated by him cannot shake off his humanity lying deep in him.

Prof. Alok Bhalla has in recent years done valuable research work on the riot stories written in different languages of South Asia. A collection of such stories in English translation titled 'Stories About the Partition of India' has recently been published in three volumes by Harper Collins Publishers in India. While reading these stories I felt that fiction writers in other South Asian Languages too share the above mentioned humanistic approach with the Pakistani writer. A comparative study of literacy writings in the different languages of South Asia may perhaps reveal to us more common points in the modes of thinking and feeling, and perhaps an acquaintance of this kind may pave the way for a better understanding at least on an intellectual level among the peoples of South Asia. This aim can best be achieved through translations from one language into another.

In Pakistan there is already a strong trend of translations from neighboring South Asian languages, more particularly from Indian languages. In recent years translations have been made of a kind, which demonstrate wish on the part of the intellectuals to have an access to the spiritual core of Indian Culture. Shanulhaq Haqqi, a distinguished Urdu scholar and poet, after translating 'Arth Shastra' attempted a translation of Gita in Urdu verse. The translation has recently been published from Karachi. Abdulaziz Khalid, a poet with an individuality of his own, made a selection from 'Maha Bharat' which after being translated in Urdu was published under the title of 'Kathan Mala'.

But perhaps the trend of translation from contemporary literature is more strong. I may refer at random to a few collections of such translations in recent years.

Bara Hindustani Shahir (Twelve Indian Poets) is a collection of Urdu translations of poems picked up from Hindi, Gujrati, Marathi, and Punjabi. A collection of Urdu translations from Hindi fiction has been presented in the form of a Special Issue of 'Aaj', a literary journal of Karachi.

Translations from Indian plays include Grish Karonard's famous play 'Tughlaq' and Vijay Tendulkar's 'Silence! The court is in session', originally written in Kannada and Marathi respectively.

As for Bangladesh, most of its writers and artists are known to Pakistan from pre-Bangladesh period. Even after separation the wish to know them on intellectual level persists among the intellectuals of Pakistan and hence the continuation of the trend of translating from Bangladeshi literature. Recently a fresh urdu translation of Waliullah's Novel with urdu title 'Lal Chadar' has been published in Lahore. Masood Ashar has recently translated three stories from Hasan Azizul Huq. Shaukat Usman's Novel 'Janani' has just been translated and is soon going to be published under the title of 'Daryabibi'. Ahmad Salem has translated a number of Bangladeshi poems in English.

Aasif Farakhi, a young writer, has devoted much time in translating from Nepalese poetry and fiction.

I may here point out that writers engaged in this sort of activity are doing it in their individual capacity with no encouragement from any Government or a non-Governmental organization or any publisher. The only exception are the attempts of 'Mah-ai-Nau', a journal published under the auspices of Government of Pakistan, which during the editorship of Kishwer Naheed had planned to present translations from the fiction and poetry of all the SAARC Countries.

So most of these translations because of being the products of the writer's individual efforts are only published in the literary journals. For the reason of lack of means they cannot be collected and published in the form of books. But doesn't the activity speak of a deep wish on the part of the Pakistanis to develop a living relationship with the creative mind of South Asia, and if encouraged, will it not help in creating an atmosphere for a better understanding between those, who at present appear estranged to each other.

This estrangement with a strong desire on both sides to go on war reminds me of a legend, which depicts a chance visit of Viyas Rishi to the Darbar of Parikshit, the grandson of Arjun. Raja Parikshit touched the feet of the grand old Rishi and said 'Maharaj, allow me to ask you a question which has been disturbing me for years'.

When permitted he asked 'among my ancestors in Kurukshetra were there on both sides of the divide noble minds possessed with great wisdom and prudence. Why did they fail to realize that war brings death and destruction in its wake'.

Viyasji sighed and said 'No body can stop from happening what is inevitable'.

Was it really a convincing reply to the distressing question raised by Parikshit. Perhaps not. Getting no convincing reply in post Kurukshetra period it is still hovering overhead in South Asia. The great sage has long passed away along with the legendary world he lived in. Now the question as directed towards the sagacious minds of today. Of course nobody can stop from happening what is inevitable. But we can try to stop from happening what perhaps is not inevitable. In the light of what has been said above let me humbly make two suggestions:

1. The establishment of a South Asian translation bureau, which may undertake to translate literary and all kinds of meaningful writings from one language to other languages of South Asia.

2. The establishment of a South Asian research centre with the purpose of comparative study of literary and art traditions of South Asia, which may help bringing out what is common among these traditions.

ANNEXURES

Annexure A

FIFTH SOUTH ASIA DIALOGUE

Venue: BRAC Conference Centre, Rajendrapur

Date: 25-27 February, 1997

List of Participants

BANGLADESH

A.F. Salahuddin Ahmed	Former Professor of History, Dhaka University
Rosie Majid Ahsan	Professor, Dept. of Geography and Environment, Dhaka University
Milia Ali	World Bank Executive and Vocalist
Tariq Ali	Trustee, *Mukti Juddha Jadughar*
Razia Khan Amin	Professor of English, Dhaka University
Anisuzzaman	Professor of Bengali, Dhaka University
Ferdous Azim	Professor of English, Dhaka University
Maleka Begum	Gender Specialist, *Gono Sahajjo Sangstha*
Debapriya Bhattacharya	Senior Research Fellow, Bangladesh Institute of Development Studies
Jamil Choudhury	Director, Centre for Policy Dialogue
Kabir Chowdhury	Professor Emeritus, Dept. of English, Dhaka University
F.R.M. Hasan	Executive Director, *Gono Sahajjo Sangstha*
Mafidul Huq	Author and Publisher
Shireen Huq	Member, *Naripakkho*
Aminul Islam	Painter and former Principal, Bangladesh College of Arts and Crafts

Nazrul Islam	Professor, Dept. of Geography and Environment, Dhaka University and Chairman, Centre for Urban Studies
Roushan Jahan	Member, *Women for Women*
Syed Jahangir	Painter
Khushi Kabir	Co-ordinator, *Nijera Kori*
Ziaur Rahman Khan	Member of Parliament
Rashed Khan Menon	Secretary General, Workers' Party
Ataur Rahman	General Secretary, *Nagorik Natyo Sampradaya*
Justice M. Habibur Rahman	Former Chief Adviser, Caretaker Government, People's Republic of Bangladesh
Mustafizur Rahman	Research Director, Centre for Policy Dialogue
Nima Rahman	Artiste
Mamunur Rashid	Director, *Aronyak Natyo Dal*
Lala Rukh Selim	Lecturer, Institute of Fine Arts, Dhaka University and Editor, *Art*
Rehman Sobhan	Executive Chairman, Centre for Policy Dialogue
Salma Sobhan	Executive Director, *Ain-O-Salish Kendro*
M. Syeduzzaman	Ex Civil Servant and former Minister of Finance
Muhammad Yunus	Managing Director, Grameen Bank
Aly Zaker	President, *Nagorik Natyo Samprodaya*
Sara Zaker	Programme and Training Secretary, *Nagorik Natyo Samprodaya*

INDIA

Shabana Azmi	Member, Rajya Sabha and Film Star and Human Rights Activist
Navnita Chadha Behera	Centre for Policy Research
Sharbari Roy Chowdhury	Sculptor and Former Director of *Kalabhaban,* Visva Bharati

Nabaneeta Deb Sen	Professor of Comparative Literature, Jadavpur University and Writer and Poet
Sonal Mansingh	Leading Exponent of Bharat Natyam
Purabi Mukharji	Programme Coordinator, India International Centre
U.R. Anantha Murthy	President, Sahitya Academy
V.A. Pai Panandiker	Director, Centre for Policy Research
Vijay Tendulkar	Theatre Director and Playwright

NEPAL

Durga P. Bhandari	Professor of English Literature, Trivuban University
Kumar Basnyat	Folk Singer and Dancer
Yadav Kharel	Poet and Writer
Devendra Raj Panday	Chairman, Nepal South Asia Centre and former Finance Minister of Nepal
Ragini Upadhayay	Painter

PAKISTAN

Sarwat Ali	Director, Gallery, National College of Arts
Naazish Ata-Ullah	Lecturer, National College of Arts
Madeeha Gauhar	Director, *Ajoka Theatre*
Iftikhar ul Haq	Secretary General, Independent Planning Commission
Mubashir Hasan	Chairman, Independent Planning Commission and former Finance Minister of Pakistan
Intazir Husain	Writer
Shahid Nadeem	General Manager, PTV Lahore and Playwright

SRI-LANKA

V. Ambalavanar	Former Secretary to the President of Sri-Lanka

M.M.K. Disanayaka	Instructor in English, University of Colombo
Sirima Kiribamune	Professor of History, University of Peradeniya and Senior Research Fellow, International Centre for Ethnic Studies
G.H. Peiris	Professor of Geography, University of Peradeniya and Senior Research Fellow, International Centre for Ethnic Studies
K.M. De Silva	Executive Director, International Centre for Ethnic Studies

Annexure B

Fifth South Asia Dialogue on Cultural Co-operation Agenda

TUESDAY
25 February 1997

09:30-10:15	**Inaugural Session** (Venue: BRAC Centre, Rajendrapur)
	Welcome Address by Prof. Rehman Sobhan, Executive Chairman, CPD
	Inaugural Address by Mr. Justice Muhammad Habibur Rahman, Former Chief, Care Taker Government and Chief Justice of Bangladesh
	Vote of thanks
10:15-10:45	Tea Break
10:45-13:00	**Working Session I** (Venue: BRAC Centre, Rajendrapur)
	Subject: **Social Justice and Human Rights**
	Presentation of papers and Discussion
13:00-14:00	Lunch break
14:00-16:45	**Working Session I** (continued)
	Discussion on papers presented at Session I
17:00	Leave for Dhaka
18:30	Visit Art Exhibition based on the Dialogue themes at the National Museum Gallery, Shahbag, Dhaka
19:00	**Cultural Programme** at the National Museum Auditorium, Shahbag, Dhaka
	i. Literary readings by Shabana Azmi on conference

ii. Excerpts of plays

a. *Mukhosh* presented by the *Nagorik Natya Sampradaya*

b. *Kokilara* presented by the *Theatre* and

c. *Pathor* presented by the *Aranyak Natya Dal*

WEDNESDAY
26 February 1997

09:30-10:45	**Working Session II** (Venue: BRAC Centre, Rajendrapur)
	Subject: **Women in Society**
	Presentation of papers
10:45-11:00	Tea break
11:00-13:00	Discussion on papers presented at Working Session II
13:00-14:00	Lunch break
14:00-16:45	**Working Session II** (continued)
	Discussion continues
16:45	Leave for Dhaka
17:30	Visit to *Muktijuddha Jadughar*
19:00	**Cultural Programme** at the National Museum Auditorium, Shahbag, Dhaka
	Tagore's Dance drama *Chandalika* staged by *Sadhana*

THURSDAY
27 February 1997

09:30-10:45	**Working Session III** (Venue: BRAC Centre, Rajendrapur)
	Subject: **Fundamentalism and Communalism**
	Presentation of papers
10:45-11:00	Tea Break
11:00-13:00	Discussion on Papers presented at the Working Session III
13:00-14:00	Lunch break
14:00-16:00	**Working Session III** (Continued)
	Discussion continues
16:00-16:45	**Concluding Session** (Venue: BRAC Centre, Rajendrapur)

17:00 Leave for Dhaka

19:00 **Cultural Programme** at the Auditorium of the Osmani Memorial Hall, Dhaka

a. Poetry, Drama and Prose readings by dialogue participants from Bangladesh, India, Nepal, Pakistan and Sri Lanka

b. Dance recital of *Draupadi* by Sonal Mansingh

Index